English Explained

English Explained

A Guide to Misunderstood and Confusing Elements of Grammar

Steve Hart

HKU
PRESS
香港大學出版社

Hong Kong University Press
The University of Hong Kong
Pokfulam Road
Hong Kong
https://hkupress.hku.hk

ISBN 978-988-8528-43-1 (*Paperback*)

British Library Cataloguing-in-Publication Data
A catalogue record for this book is available from the British Library.

10 9 8 7 6 5 4 3 2 1

Printed and bound by Hang Tai Printing Co., Ltd. in Hong Kong, China

CONTENTS

C. PREPOSITIONS, ADJECTIVES, AND ADVERBS

D. SUBJECT, CLAUSES, AND QUESTIONS

ANNOTATED CONTENTS

KEY TO SYMBOLS

* Ungrammatical: An example that contains a grammar error.
  e.g.   *I have begin.*

† Speech: An example that is likely to be spoken.
  e.g.   *Did you see it?* †

INTRODUCTION

English is a frustrating language that rarely sticks to its own rules. To make matters worse, some of the 'rules' we are taught are not genuine rules at all. Add to the mix a host of idiomatic phrases and the natural idiosyncrasies that arise from hundreds of years of evolution (or stagnation) and it is no real surprise we are often left bewildered and confused by English and its grammar.

A cursory glance at a random set of English phrases and sentences will, likely, reveal that the guidelines upon which most learners of English depend, and most language school grammar sessions are based, really cannot be trusted. And even the tried and tested rules have exceptions; in fact, sometimes there are exceptions to the exceptions! The purpose of *English Explained* is to present these areas of English most affected by misinformation and confusion.

This book has been written in the first instance for teachers or prospective teachers of English whose first language is not English. But it will also appeal to any student who seeks a better grasp and understanding of English grammar—essential for achieving competency in both writing and reading.

The problem with many reference books is that they give rather narrow overviews of each grammar area and address only the standard practices. This leads learners to assume anything outside of this is incorrect usage. To address the problem, the fifty sections of *English Explained* cover the misunderstood, the misleading, and anything that a learner's ear or eye would consider atypical. This means that, while some exceptions to a grammar rule or to the familiar usage are covered, there are also many examples that are simply irregular forms or variations to the common usage (but crucially, examples that speakers of English whose first language is not English may well consider to be erroneous).

English Explained has been designed to assist both students and teachers, especially on a practical level. Students relying on apps and software to check grammar still need a good grasp of the language to assess whether the suggestions should be followed or the warnings heeded. And teachers instructing students of various abilities will need to fill the gaps in their grammar knowledge to avoid being asked questions for which they can provide no answer. As the ultimate recipients of the information in this book will be students and teachers who are learning their craft, some of the more indulgent or exclusive vernacular common in linguistic texts has been overlooked where possible for more practical and instructive terms.

One key aim of *English Explained* is to equip teachers with the knowledge and the awareness to answer any challenging questions that enquiring minds might pose over the course of an English class. For instance, it will not take long for a bright student to come up with examples that disprove the following:

A sentence cannot end with a preposition.

They is a plural-only pronoun.

Determiners always come before other modifiers.

Nouns must take definite articles when mentioned a second time.

Infinitives should not be split.

Although it is undoubtedly beneficial to language learners, the impact of the increasing standardisation of English does lead to a loss of understanding of word origins. This standardisation has the knock-on effect of making the elements that have not undergone a change appear even more curious and illogical to those whose first language is not English.

It is these curious and illogical elements, then, that are explored over the next 170 pages. And whether you are a teacher of the language or a student, after acquiring the necessary knowledge from the pages of *English Explained* you'll be able to confidently answer any grammar query—no matter how seemingly complex or obscure—raised in your classroom.

Steve Hart
2019

CHAPTER FORMAT

Chapter title

Curious capitalisation

Introduction—general grammar points

An initial capital letter indicates that a word is a proper noun . . .

Example(s)—contrary and confusing examples

(5) We are all seekers of the Truth.

Student enquiry—questions a learner may have about the examples

I know that capital letters should be used when words are proper nouns, but . . .

Explanation—answers to those questions and further exploration of the point(s)

An initial capital indicates that a noun is naming something . . .

And another thing . . . —other related points of interest

Prefixes that are attached to proper nouns are not capitalised.

A. NOUN, NUMBER, AND DETERMINER

1
Curious capitalisation

An initial capital letter indicates that a word is a proper noun (unless the word begins a sentence, in which case it must have a capital but may not be a proper noun). A proper noun identifies the name of a person, place or organisation.

Emily Leung   *Thailand*   *Maitland Industries*

Words derived from proper nouns, such as their adjective forms, will also require initial capitals.

Marxist   *Swedish*   *Dickensian*

Geographical features and political divisions of land are familiar to most as terms that will require initial capital letters (*Gobi Desert, Atlantic Ocean, North Dakota*). Perhaps less evident is that some historical events and institutions will also need them.

the Great Plague   *the Second World War*   *the House of Lords*

—To demonstrate the distinction between a proper and a common noun, example (1) provides two instances of the noun *university*. The first instance represents part of the name of a specific institution (meaning it is a proper noun and therefore is capitalised). The second instance is also referring to a specific university but is not stating the name of the institution (meaning it is a common noun and therefore should be lower case).

> *The <u>University</u> of Hong Kong is now part of this scheme. Another <u>university</u>*
> *has also shown some interest.*   (1)

—Initial capitals can be used on words appearing in titles and headings. It is customary to keep any prepositions, co-ordinators or articles lower case.

> *Implementing <u>a</u> New Primary Chinese Curriculum: Impact <u>on</u> Learning*
> *Outcomes <u>within a</u> Small Rural School.*   (2)

> *Internet Regulation <u>in</u> Japan <u>after the</u> 2000s.*   (3)

> *Table 3: Education Deprivation <u>by</u> Age <u>and</u> Disability.*   (4)

◆ ◆ ◆

(5) We are all seekers of the Truth.

(6) The depiction of Death with a scythe grew from this tradition.

Student enquiry: I know that capital letters should be used when words are proper nouns, but I sometimes see nouns other than names and places given initial capitals. For example, what is the reason for common nouns like *truth* and *death* being given capitals, as in (5) and (6)?

Explanation

An initial capital indicates that a noun is naming something and is therefore a unique reference. But situations do arise when common nouns are given proper-noun status. Concepts such as *truth, beauty, time, death* and *fate* can take initial capitals in certain circumstances, usually when the absolute or principal version of the idea is meant by the writer. There is often an element of personification (when human qualities are given to non-human subjects) and symbolism to this usage, as is apparent in (6).

Care should be taken with this practice of capitalisation because it is more a literary device suited to fiction and poetry, and the nouns able to take a capital in this way are few.

And another thing . . . 1

Prefixes that are attached to proper nouns are not capitalised.

Most of these buildings are <u>pre</u>-Victorian.

Their later work reflected this <u>anti</u>-Hollywood stance.

When the prefix derives from a proper noun, though, initial capitals should be used for both parts.

It is a <u>Sino</u>-Vietnamese word meaning 'comfort'.

This was a key period for <u>Anglo</u>-Irish relations.

2
Nouns with changing countability

A countable noun can, unsurprisingly, appear after the determiners *a, three*, and *many*. And because the noun *doctor* is countable, we can write *a doctor, three doctors* and *many doctors*. Likewise, the noun *evidence* is uncountable, cannot be made plural, and for this reason **an evidence, *three evidences* and **many evidences* are incorrect forms.

Associated with countability is the concept of boundedness. The idea is that a countable noun is countable because it has a clear boundary that will mark it out as an entity with a clear beginning and an end (although not necessarily in a physical or tangible sense). Uncountable nouns are unbounded and viewed as a unit or mass with no potential for division; they cannot be separated like countable nouns. Despite the distinction, it is not always easy to categorise nouns as definitively one or the other. There are four areas of interest here:

~1: some typically countable nouns can receive mass (uncountable) interpretations.

A ballet is a countable activity. But when reference is made to the dance form in general terms, it takes on an uncountable meaning (1ii).

> In a distinguished career he wrote seventeen <u>ballets</u> for the company.　　(1i)

> His daughter also studied <u>ballet</u>.　　(1ii)

In this next example, the uncountable instance of *paper* (2i) is referring to the material. The countable instance is the functional product, i.e. written documents that traditionally consisted of sheets of the material (2ii) (which can now be electronic in origin).

> It needs to be written on <u>paper</u>.　　(2i)

> She has published several <u>papers</u> recently.　　(2ii)

In (3i), the uncountable noun refers to space in general; in (3ii), the plural indicates specific areas or spaces.

> We don't have <u>room</u> for them currently.　　(3i)

> The second floor has three meeting <u>rooms</u>.　　(3ii)

We can see, then, a relationship between the general idea, element or material (the uncountable instance) and a specific case or example of it (the countable instance).

~2: some nouns widely regarded as uncountable can be used in a countable way with an indefinite article (4i) but lack a plural form (4ii).

In (4i), an uncountable noun takes an indefinite article for an instance of the concept or a type.

A greater appreciation for nature is the outcome of all of this.   (4i)

*They need to show some appreciations.   (4ii)

This practice is more common than one might think. Here, *knowledge* is the uncountable noun used with the indefinite article.

It was a knowledge that would prove vital in her new career.   (5)

~3: some uncountable nouns appear to have countable equivalents but they are, in fact, unrelated.

Here are two instances of the noun *depression*. But they are unconnected words and have independent meanings.

There is no suggestion that depression is a factor.   (6i)

The course was disrupted by two large depressions in the road.   (6ii)

~4: some nouns are found only in the plural.

The nouns underlined in (7) and (8) have no singular form.

The proceeds went to a local charity.   (7)

Some of the clothes on display were from an earlier collection.   (8)

—There is a lack of clarity about certain nouns. Some consider *data* to be singular, while others use it as a plural (the latter group acknowledging a singular form, *datum*). *News* and *politics* appear plural in form but in (9) and (10) take a singular demonstrative (*this*) and a singular verb (*is*) respectively, which is true of many fields of study and sports (e.g. *economics, mathematics, athletics*).

I received this news on Friday.   (**I received these news on Friday.*)   (9)

Politics is unlikely to be a reason for this.   (**Politics are . . .*)   (10)

◆ ◆ ◆

(11) Certain behaviours are considered 'programmed'.

(12) Several of these injustices were highlighted in the report.

(13) He evidences this in the second section of the document.

Student enquiry: The nouns in (11), (12) and (13) are all uncountable (*behaviour, (in)justice and evidence*) and yet they have plural forms in these examples. I didn't know that an uncountable noun could be split up, as it is considered a mass. This usage is even more surprising given that the examples seem to be abstract nouns. If they are concepts, how can they be plural?

Explanation

Examples (11) and (12) do contain concept nouns, but sometimes these nouns can be used to refer to specific instances of the idea or the notion (in our examples, *behaviours* that somebody has shown and *injustices* that have come to light). Concept nouns with this bounded or divisible interpretation are prolific in the human sciences and in the terminology of legal studies. In (11), then, the typically uncountable noun *behaviour* has a countable reading and takes a plural. Here are some further examples.

> *They often display <u>behaviours</u> that we would consider atypical.*   (14)

> *The next step is to work out the <u>incomes</u> of these employees.*   (15)

> *Different <u>energies</u> act upon the body in different ways.*   (16)

Some uncountable nouns cannot be made plural, but this capability for division may still apply. They must rely on a partitive phrase such as *piece of* or *type of* or expressions like *a period of* to represent these instances of the noun. It is therefore inaccurate to explicitly say that mass or uncountable nouns cannot be divided up. *Information* is one such uncountable noun that has no plural capacity. It relies on a partitive phrase.

> *There are certain <u>types of</u> information that should remain classified.*   (17)

> **There are certain informations . . .*

(13) is actually a verb in the third person singular and does not relate to this discussion. It is a common mistake to make. *Evidence* can be both a noun (*a piece of evidence*) and a verb (*I am able to evidence this*).

And another thing . . . 2

We saw uncountable nouns taking indefinite articles earlier. Well, even some plural nouns can receive them.

> *They suggested that we store the historical records in <u>an archives</u>.*

3

Quantities that do not add up

The plural form of a noun usually differs from the singular by inflection (often of the ending). These inflections are commonly *s*, *es*, or *ies*.

hundred   hundreds   *box boxes*   *commentary   commentaries*

Words of Latin, Greek or French origin may well deviate from the typical endings.

alumnus   alumni   *appendix   appendices*   *chateau   chateaux*

genus   genera   *phenomenon   phenomena*   *stratum   strata*

—Singular nouns that end in *f* or *fe* may change to *ves* in the plural

one <u>half</u>   *a <u>leaf</u>*   *one <u>life</u>*

two <u>halves</u>   *these <u>leaves</u>*   *several <u>lives</u>*

or take a standard *s* ending.

the <u>chief</u>   *a <u>cliff</u>*   *this <u>safe</u>*

village <u>chiefs</u>   *below the <u>cliffs</u>*   *empty <u>safes</u>*

—There are also irregular plurals in which the change occurs through an internal vowel instead of a change to the ending.

man   men   *woman   women*   *tooth   teeth*   *foot   feet*

—A key area of English grammar is subject-verb agreement. A singular subject takes a singular verb form (1i); a plural subject requires a plural verb (1ii).

<u>A dress is</u> required to be worn for this function.   (1i)

<u>Dresses are</u> required to be worn for this function.   (1ii)

◆   ◆   ◆

(2) Four hundred will be affected by this scheme.

(3) Several thousand are expected to take part.

(4) We were also informed that £10,000 was our limit.

Student enquiry: Why are *hundred* and *thousand* not written as plurals in (2) and (3) when the units of reference are clearly multiples (*four* and *several*)? And example (4) seems to break the subject-verb agreement rule because 10,000 is a plural amount and yet the verb remains singular (*was*).

Explanation

When a unit relating to number, value or dimension is acting as a modifier, it is written in the singular form even if there is a number greater than one preceding it (5i).

It is a seven-<u>storey</u> building. (5i)

When that unit is the head noun and being modified itself, it will agree with the plurality of the modifier as expected.

The building has seven <u>storeys</u>. (5ii)

But when the units *hundred, thousand* and *million* are preceded by a number, they stay singular in form. This is why in (2) and (3), although they occur with numbers greater than 1, they are not written as plurals.

When not preceded by a quantity phrase, the expected plural form will be used (6).

<u>Thousands</u> of workers will be able to take advantage of this from next week.   (6)

In some regional dialects the plural form may, rather surprisingly, be abandoned.

It is close to four <u>foot</u>.† (7)

Not long, maybe three <u>month</u> away.† (8)

The issue in (4) relates to subject-verb agreement. The money (*£10,000*) is considered a collective (and so single) amount and takes a singular verb. Measurements of distance or time will also take singular verb forms even if they are greater in value than one.

Four hours <u>is</u> a long time to wait. (9)

I have been warned that <u>26 miles is</u> a considerable distance for a novice! (10)

And another thing . . . 3

Plants, vegetables and certain animals (especially those hunted for food and for sport) can take a singular form when their value is greater than one and a plural would be expected. This is known as collectivising (see **Glossary**).

The recipe requires four <u>cauliflower</u> and a radish.

I heard them boast about having shot three <u>pheasant</u>.†

The reason they are singular is that in these situations they are not considered individual animals or vegetables but instead seen as a recognised set, i.e. a collective type.

4

Collective divisions?

Collective nouns (and terms of a similar nature) are seen as containing individual members that, together, represent a unit or set. Because they are viewed as a single entity, they require a singular verb.

Group C was given the original test paper. (1)

The Academic Board meets fortnightly. (2)

Group C in (1) is likely to have a membership of more than one, but the group is considered a single unit and so is followed by a singular verb form. As well as people, collective nouns are used to name groups of animals (3), places (4) and ideas (5).

The herd was approaching the village. (3)

This band of cities is considered in need of development. (4)

Another set of approaches has been developed by Matthews (2002). (5)

◆ ◆ ◆

(6) The agency consists of five consultants and two negotiators. There are plans to expand the business although the agency are divided on which region to enter.

Student enquiry: In example (6), there are two instances of the noun *agency*. The first time it appears it takes a singular verb form, but the second time it takes a plural. I think I have also seen this variation with the nouns *committee* and *government*. If it is a collective noun, then it should be singular. And if there is a choice, surely there needs to be consistency rather than a singular verb and a plural verb being employed in the same paragraph for the same noun reference.

Explanation

Although collective nouns are generally considered singular, the agreement rule may be broken when the focus is not on the group as a whole but on the individual members; consider a scenario in which the collective is not unified on an issue or there is a group within the group that is acting differently or has a contrary viewpoint to the others. This is the explanation for (6), where the first instance of *agency* is in the collective (single unit) sense and the second instance indicates differences within the group (that there is no consensus on where to move to). This distinction can be illustrated by trying to use a plural with the first instance of the noun.

*The agency <u>consist</u> of five consultants and two negotiators. (7)

This does not work because the information applies to the group as a whole: it is detailing the structure of the agency. The plural form, then, has the effect of moving the attention towards individuals within the group (often because not all members are united or behaving in the same way). Collectivising, as was seen in **3**, does the opposite and puts the focus onto the collective.

And another thing . . . 4

American English is less likely to employ the plural verb, preferring to retain the standard agreement rule for collective nouns (unless there is an obvious focus on individual members of the group or internal factions).

In sports reporting, there is a notable discrepancy between American English (AmE) and British English (BrE).

BrE will ignore the collective nature of the noun.

<u>Tottenham</u> <u>have</u> won their previous two matches at the stadium.

AmE will recognise it even if the team name is plural.

<u>New York Red Bulls</u> <u>has</u> the chance to go top with a win today.

5
The singular elements of a compound

Compound nouns are made up of at least two elements. They can appear as one word (*underground*), two words (*car park*) or hyphenated (*vice-president*). The selection of a hyphen may be made to avoid ambiguity (noticeably in *small-business executives* and potentially in *vice-president* above). And this is often the reason for hyphenating compound adjectives. The choice between one word, two words or hyphen may also depend on how recognised and ingrained the term has become in the language (the one-word version being fully ingrained and the hyphenated one in a state of flux). This next compound has progressed to the stage where it is now most likely to be written as one word.

life style   life-style   lifestyle

—There is a tendency to place hyphens between countries and regions with two parts to their name, and to use them for adjective forms.

Journalists that have reported this issue are mainly Middle-Eastern. (1)

But often these are not true compounds. Phrases of this nature will usually only require hyphens when they feature a shortened form of the country or region (see also **1**).

The roots of Greco-Roman wrestling are explored in this first article. (2)

—When two-word compounds contain two nouns, one will be modifying and the other will be in the head position. Some nouns in the modifying (initial) position act more like adjectives; when this is the case, the head noun is likely to be stressed or emphasised when spoken.

She began working in the industry as a child star. (3)

When neither of the nouns is considered the head and they have equal weight, the modifier may be stressed or the stress may be neutral.

They also deal with cases of child abuse. (4)

The difference between the two forms is apparent when attempting to turn them into possessive phrases. Only (4) (the one with equal stress or modifier stress) can be converted.

child star (3)   *The star of a child   *a child's star

child abuse (4)   The abuse of a child   a child's abuse

—Pronunciation is key to differentiating a compound noun (5i) from a phrase that features the same words but does not have this union (5ii).

Rainfall tends to increase this time of year.   (5i)

I'm here watching the rain fall.†   (5ii)

In (5i), the stress falls on the first part of the noun. But the same phrase in (5ii) is not a compound, just two distinct words with a natural pause in between.

In compound adjectives the stress will fall on the second part (6), as it did in (3) when the first noun of the compound was acting like an adjective.

I found the methods a little old-fashioned.   (6)

—Stress and intonation are crucial for those phrases at risk from ambiguity. Here in (7i), stress on the modifier implies the tutor teaches English. In (7ii), the stress on the head or a neutral intonation implies the tutor is English, i.e. has English nationality, but may not teach the language.

An English tutor   (7i)

An English tutor   (7ii)

◆ ◆ ◆

(8) They were instructed to scissor-cut these garments.

(9) This led to another arms race between the two nations.

(10) We can witness this in the earnings reviews.

Student enquiry: When a compound is made plural, I never know whether to put the *s* on the first part or the second. And then there are examples like (8) where a verb contains a plural-only noun (*scissors*) but it is written in the singular. In (9), the plural is on the first noun. But if *arms* is plural in (9), I would expect *scissors* in (8) to be as well because they are both plural-only words. And then in (10), both parts of the noun phrase are plural!

Explanation

The more significant word in the compound or the one that changes in number tends to take the plural form. The much-cited American example *chiefs of staff* demonstrates this. The plural-only noun *scissors* is singular in (8) because it has an equivalent singular verb form (*to scissor*). But the plural-only noun *arms* will retain its form as seen in (9).

(10) contains a modifier (*earnings*) that is characteristically plural. And it remains plural when the phrase it is a part of is also plural. The outcome is two inflected words. Other examples include *goods* and *systems*.

These <u>goods standards</u> relate only to the European Union.   (11)

The article looks at <u>systems approaches</u> for risk management.   (12)

There is also no merit in the assertion that only irregular plurals can act as the modifier in a compound. There are countless examples, including those above, demonstrating that regular plurals (those with a standard way of forming the plural, such as adding *s* or *es*) can fulfil the role of modifier.

<u>Careers</u> Service   <u>Festivities</u> Coordinator

And another thing . . . 5

The form of certain plural nouns ending in *-ful* can show variation. The traditional method was for the *s* to appear before the suffix; increasingly, it is being placed after it.

Seven bucketsful of water   Seven bucketfuls of water

Three mouthsful for each child   Three mouthfuls for each child

6

Possessing a choice

We saw in **5** that nouns can be modified by adjectives (1, 2) or by other nouns (3).

A French designer won the award. (1)

The damaged painting was removed from the exhibition. (2)

The book review was complimentary. (3)

—When association or possession occurs, the writer sometimes has a free choice between an apostrophe and an *of*-phrase.

The accent of the teacher can also be a barrier. (4)

The teacher's accent can also be a barrier. (5)

Often, though, only one form will be appropriate. When the noun has a human or personal reference (6), the apostrophe form is often preferred. Otherwise, the *of*-form is likely to be required (7).

John's project was due in on Monday.† (*The project of John*) (6)

The length of the speech was another factor. (*The speech's length*) (7)

Typically, the *of*-form will have an abstract noun and an impersonal reference, and the apostrophe form will contain a proper noun and a personal one. That said, a noun with a non-human reference can still take an apostrophe form.

The film's takings were affected by the good weather that month. (8)

—Sometimes, neither of these options are available and a compound noun is applied instead.

The office party has been cancelled. (9)

**The office's party* **The party of the office*

In (10), the reference is impersonal and has a neutral tone because it is not any particular student's garden; thus, the compound is chosen.

The student garden has also been redesigned for the new term. (10)

—From a semantic (see **Glossary**) perspective, an *of*-phrase is usually associated with new information, whereas the apostrophe form is likely to relate to something or someone already mentioned.

The appointment of Mike Matthews has raised the profile of the club ... and Mike's appointment will allow the trainers to pursue other projects. (11)

◆ ◆ ◆

(12) We can now get the opinions of Judy Chen on this matter.†

(13i) The instructor in the first training session's delivery was very slow.

(14) You can watch this in the month of December.

Student enquiry: I was wondering why example (12) does not have the possessive apostrophe, as it is relating to a person's opinions. In (13i), is it OK for the apostrophe to be so far away from the head noun? (14) sounds quite wordy, but I realise that the apostrophe is not an option here, so I assume this does need an *of*-phrase.

Explanation

In (12), an *of*-phrase has been selected because, in all likelihood, the person has yet to be introduced. Either that or the speaker has decided to use a more formal tone, which an *of*-phrase can achieve.

(13i) does contain a lengthy gap between the head noun and the apostrophe, and this would only really be acceptable in informal writing. The closer the apostrophe is to the head noun the better, because otherwise the reader may not be able to follow the reference (i.e. to whom the possession is referring). A better construction for (13i) might be

The instructor's delivery in the first training session was very slow. (13ii)

That said, there are instances when a gap is required between the initial noun and the possessive apostrophe.

We can see it in Emily and her carer's relationship. (15)

When two nouns are separated by *of* and both nouns are considered to have equal weighting, there will be no apostrophe form equivalent. The nouns are called appositives (see **Glossary**), and it is evidenced in (14) with **December's month* not being a valid substitute for *the month of December*.

Another time the possessive apostrophe is unavailable is when the two elements of the *of*-phrase are considered partitive, or parts of a whole.

> A <u>piece of advice</u>, I wouldn't walk in there just yet.†   (16)

> *An advice's piece . . .*

And another thing . . . 6

The so-called double genitive (see also **Glossary**) is a phrase that contains both an *of*-phrase and a possessive apostrophe. Sometimes, the reason is syntactic (here, because *The Duke of Norfolk* is a title).

> *The Duke of Norfolk's cousin arrives tomorrow.*†

Other times, the double genitive is required to help aid understanding. In this example it changes the meaning of the sentence.

> *The exhibition contains photos of the prince.*

> *The exhibition contains photos of the prince's.*

In the former, there are photos in the exhibition that feature the prince. In the latter, there are photos taken by or owned by the prince but that are not necessarily of him.

Another interesting possessive construction is in the form of a (noun)'s (noun).

> *She is thought of as a poet's poet.*

There is a misconception arising from this type of construction in that some believe it refers to (using the example above) the 'best of all' poets; what it actually means is that you might have to be a poet yourself to fully appreciate her.

7
Determining an order

Determiners are words that introduce or identify nouns. The class contains the following subcategories:

articles—the, a/an   demonstratives—this, that, these, those . . .

possessives—my, its, our, their . . . quantifiers—all, some, many, few . . .

Determiners will come before other modifiers of the head word to provide information on, among other things, definiteness, countability and number.

DETERMINER MODIFIER HEAD

| *These* | *young* | *learners* | *exceeded our expectations.* | (1) |
| *The* | *second* | *report* | *did contain this information.* | (2) |

♦ ♦ ♦

(3) Unfortunately, this was too small a range for any meaningful results.

(4) This raises the question of how obvious a fault must be before it is identified.

Student enquiry: I know that an article, as a determiner, must come before the noun and before any words modifying the noun. And yet in examples (3) and (4), the articles appear AFTER the modifying term. Usually, the noun phrases here would be written: *a small range* and *an obvious fault*. So, how are these phrases in (3) and (4) correct in light of the rule that determiners come before modifiers? And if they are, does the position of the indefinite article affect the meaning at all?

Explanation

Determiners will ordinarily come before any modifiers of the noun in a sentence, but there are, unsurprisingly, exceptions. Clauses that begin with the words *too* (3,6), *how* (4) and *so* (5) can have a different form whereby the order of the words is reversed. The determiner in these phrases is often an indefinite article (*a/an*). The next examples will serve as illustration.

A useful experience = *This proved to be <u>so useful an experience</u> that all departments were encouraged to take part.* (5)

A good offer = *It was <u>too good an offer</u> to turn down.* (6)

The order in which the elements occur is as follows:

('How/Too/So' modifier) (determiner) (noun head)

And another thing . . . 7

When determiners appear next to each other there is sometimes a fixed order (although some will require an *of*-phrase to co-exist). For instance, *all* and *both* come before articles and demonstratives when preceding noun phrases.

<u>All these</u> changes will significantly impact the environment.

<u>Both those</u> issues were raised in the meeting.

Many appears after demonstratives and the definite article. But it can also occur before the indefinite article. As a determiner, *more* comes before both types of article.

These <u>many</u> evolutions have been documented by Morgan (2017).

<u>Many an</u> issue can be solved this way.

It is <u>more the</u> student than the teacher in this situation.

It was <u>more an</u> inconvenience than a real setback.

Most and *much* tend to stand alone as determiners (but can take articles when they are adverbs).

<u>Most</u> employees will be offered some form of counselling.

<u>Much</u> information has already been provided on this.

8
The strong and the weak determiner

Some determiners can be used with either a singular or a plural noun; others are restricted to singular only or plural only. *Another* occurs with singular nouns.

> *Another reason is the cost involved.* (1)

Those is used with plurals.

> *Fortunately, those problems are behind us now.* (2)

—As seen in **7**, more than one determiner can appear in a sentence. However, the determiners *each, some* and *any* cannot combine with other members of the class. An *of*-phrase would need to be added.

> **These some issues can be addressed at a later time.* (3)

(Some of these issues …)

> **It is available in any those states.* (4)

(… any of those states).

◆ ◆ ◆

(5) There was some fault with the coding of the program.

(6) Some teacher was looking at it yesterday, I seem to remember.†

(7) We will happily address any issue.

Student enquiry: I would expect *some* to be used with a plural noun because it has a plural meaning. But it occurs with singular countable nouns in (5) and (6). The phrase *some teacher*, for instance, I am unsure about. I am also surprised that *any* is used with a singular countable noun in (7). It seems logical that *any* would be used with uncountable nouns and plurals. For instance, you cannot say, *Are there any problem with the new system?*. You have to use the plural form *problems*.

Explanation

The quantifiers *some* and *any* have several functions, one of which relates to an unaccented or weak form. The unaccented version of *some* is used with plural and uncountable nouns and has a mass interpretation. It is the form that the student was expecting to see in (5) and (6).

There are some students here to see the tutor.†   (8)

Often the word is clipped or shortened when spoken.

When *some* is used in its strong or accented form, however, it refers to an individual person or object and therefore does not relate to an amount—hence the singular nouns in (5) and (6). It is pronounced fully and even emphasised in this case. In (5), it means an unidentified fault, and in (6) it means a particular teacher. There are other uses of *some*. In informal English, it can be used as an intensifier to express strong emotion about something.

It was some performance by her.   (9)

Some can also be employed before a number for an approximation that is equivalent to *about*.

Some fifty students were protesting outside the gates.   (10)

Any also has strong and weak forms. The strong form allows it to be used with singular, plural and uncountable nouns. It has the meaning of 'it does not matter which' in (7) and here in (11).

The participants could pick any container.   (11)

The weak or unaccented form refers to an indefinite quantity. It would not occur with singular nouns when used in this way. This is the form that is familiar to the student making the enquiry.

Are there any questions? †   (12)

And another thing . . . 8

It is worth bearing in mind that when *any* and *some* occur in sentences with a negative connotation, they can lose their quantity status and stand for zero or none.

We were unable to find any locations suitable to carry out this task.

Only four of the participants refused to take some home with them.

9

Approximate coordination

Coordination involves two or more phrases or clauses that are joined by coordinators (also known as coordinating conjunctions). Often there is a parallel relationship between the two (or more) parts that are linked. The coordinator tends to introduce the final term.

The facilitators observed <u>and</u> made notes. (1)

We could use all the items <u>or</u> a select few. (2)

The two examples above contain the most versatile and familiar members of the coordinator class (others include *but, either, both, neither/nor*). These words link noun phrases, adjectives, modals, prepositions and various types of clause.

The circumstances are changing <u>and</u> quickly. (3)

He may <u>or</u> may not. (4)

—There is a misguided belief that coordinators can only link words or phrases of the same type (nouns with nouns, adjectives with adjectives). Example (3) certainly indicates otherwise.

Ambiguity can arise if the scope of the coordination is not clear.

Take the notes from the desk <u>and</u> the report to the other department. (5)

The young researcher <u>and</u> assistant had almost finished the paper. (6)

In (5) it is unclear whether the instruction is to pick the notes up from the desk and then take the report to the other department (but not necessarily give the notes to the department as well) or to take both the notes and the report to the other department. In (6), one reading is that the young researcher is also the assistant; the other is that there are two people working on the paper.

—The coordinator *or* can indicate alternatives (7), with or without *either*. It can also represent uncertainty (8).

You can buy it (either) hot or cold. (7)

Did they say hot or cold? † (8)

◆ ◆ ◆

(9) A: 'Well, there were 20 or 30 guidelines in the document.'

    B: 'Yes, we counted 25 in total.'

    A: 'I thought so.'†

Student enquiry: From the short dialogue in (9), I am unsure about Speaker A's reaction to being told there were 25 guidelines and also Speaker B's initial affirmative response. Speaker A thought there were 20 or 30, so why, on hearing that there were 25 guidelines, did they consider themselves to be correct or at least not surprised?

Explanation

Sometimes the coordinator *or* can be used between numbers to provide approximations rather than two explicit options. By saying 20 or 30 (9), an approximation of BETWEEN 20 and 30 was meant by Speaker A, not exactly 20 or exactly 30. This can be inferred from the response to hearing that there were 25. This number is between 20 and 30, so Speaker A's approximation was accurate. It is also possible for this phrase not to represent an approximation, though. In (10), the speaker does mean either exactly 20 or exactly 30.

    We decided on 20 or 30 in a group. I can't remember which now.†   (10)

If the speaker received an answer of 25 here, they would be surprised.

The accuracy of the approximation is called into question when, say, *one or two* or *five or six* is stated, as the range might actually fall outside those numbers. These are vague phrases used to indicate a small number, not necessarily a strict range. The former could be referring to upwards of 4 and the latter potentially anything up to about 10. But these approximations cannot be created with any pair. Ranges tend to contain round numbers like 10, 20 and 30 or those halfway between like 15, 25, 35 instead of, say, 12, 17 and 36. Consequently, the following pairs would not be considered ranges and would instead have literal meanings.

    11 or 14   18 or 118   301 or 321

Using the terms *between . . . and . . .* would make it clearer to the reader or listener when it is meant to be an approximate range rather than a choice between two amounts.

And another thing . . . 9

Coordination with *and* usually results in a plural verb form because there are two or more constituents. But we need to be sure that there are two elements in the coordination. Here, only one entity is being referred to.

The red and white model was released in 2011.

If there are two constituents, then naturally the verb should match.

The red model and the white model are due to be updated.

Sometimes, though, the two parts are considered a single unit containing the same reference. Here, the singular verb is employed for this reason.

This divided region and source of irritation for the government was deemed a priority by the opposition parties.

10

We, meaning *me* or *you* or *us*

Pronouns are said to function as replacements for nouns or noun phrases in a sentence. They can relate to number, i.e. singular (*I*, *he/she*) and plural (*we*, *they*), and to person, wherein they identify the speaker (first person = *I*, *we*), the addressee (second person = *you*) or others (third person = *he*, *she*, *it*, *they* . . .) during an act of communication. They can refer to something or someone mentioned earlier in the text or conversation; if they do not, then the reference should be clear from the situation. In (1), the singular pronoun is replacing the noun *Harry*, who was mentioned earlier in the sentence. In (2), the plural pronoun relates to both the previously mentioned *Harry* and the narrator.

Harry was there and <u>he</u> enjoyed himself too.†	(1)
Harry was there and <u>we</u> spoke for quite a while.†	(2)

◆ ◆ ◆

(3) Professor: We understand your situation; therefore, an extension of two weeks has been granted.†

(4) We have a tendency to devalue things that come to us easily.

Student enquiry: In (3), the professor is using the plural pronoun *we* when talking to his student. As an individual person, should the professor not be using the singular *I* ? And in (4), how do we know who *we* is referring to if there is no prior reference and nothing taking place to suggest a possible actor(s)? Is *we* the narrator and somebody else?

Explanation

One reason why an individual may choose to use *we* is for speaking on behalf of an organisation or a profession. And (3) is demonstrating this exclusive sense of *we*. It can be used to show support and understanding, as it tends to soften the nature of the information given.

A writer may also use *we* in an inclusive sense to refer generically to something that all humans share, such as a common past or the current understanding of something. And this is the reason for its use in (4).

This generic form of a pronoun can also occur with *you* and *they*. In (5), reference is being made to the relevant, but unknown, people in charge.

It would help if they could decide whether to repair it or demolish it.   (5)

Here in (6), an author or expert is explaining something based on the shared knowledge from their discipline.

We tend to restrict the use of these chemicals in the early stages.   (6)

Inclusive *we* can feature in the author/reader relationship with the equivalent meaning of *you* or *you and I*.

As we can see from Figure 3 . . .   (7)

A rather formal and expressive use of *we* in spoken English is a reference that, again, can substitute for *you*.

We are looking professional today. What is the occasion? †   (8)

And another thing . . . 10

Although pronouns are said to replace nouns in a sentence, there are some instances when this is perhaps not an accurate evaluation. Indefinite pronouns like *anything, everything* and *nothing* do not substitute for nouns in the way the personal pronouns clearly do in (1) and (2). Equally, the dummy subject (see **48**) in the second example below cannot be said to be replacing an implied or previously mentioned noun.

They turned up yesterday. Everything went from the property.

It was a pupil who discovered the original document.

11
The individual pronoun problem

Personal pronouns in English can be divided into singular and plural forms.

Singular: *I, you, he, she, it*   Plural: *we, they*

Several options are available in the third person singular (1), but the only third person plural pronoun is *they* (2).

<u>He/She/It</u> *influenced the outcome significantly.* (1)

<u>They</u> *can visit us next week.*† (2)

—Possessive determiners come before the noun and include *my, your, his, her, our,* and *their.*

We need <u>their</u> report by Friday. (3)

—Possessive pronouns can also be categorised as singular or plural and are used instead of a noun/noun phrase.

Singular: *mine, yours, his, hers*   Plural: *ours, theirs*

<u>Theirs</u> *(Their report) should also contain the annual figures.* (4)

◆ ◆ ◆

(5) A manager will have to meet their targets if they are to remain in the job.

(6) If someone has a solution, they should inform their group leader immediately.

Student enquiry: *They* is a plural pronoun and *their* is a plural possessive determiner, yet in (5) and (6) they appear to be referring to singular nouns. The subjects in these sentences are *a manager* and *someone*, both individuals. Should the appropriate forms not be *he/she* and *his/her*?

Explanation

There is much debate as to whether *they* is appropriate when referring to an individual. Some writers may opt for the slightly awkward *he/she* form to keep the gender neutral when the reference is generic (no individual in mind) or to conceal the gender of the subject if the individual is known. Now, the writer in (5) has employed *they* to refer to a (though no particular) manager. This is common practice.

Here, then, are the available options:

A *manager should ensure that he/she has instructed his/her team by Friday so he/she/they can pass the inspection.* (7i)

A *manager should ensure that they have instructed their team by Friday so they can pass the inspection.* (7ii)

Note that a plural verb (*have*) is still required in (7ii) when using *they* to refer to an individual. Some would view this example to be grammatically incorrect because the plural pronoun does not agree with the singular subject it refers to. But with no suitable singular pronoun to do this job and *one* seen as too pompous for the role, *they* has stepped in to fill this gap in the grammar (although there is plenty of evidence indicating that *they* has been used in this way for hundreds of years). Besides, and as (7i) highlights, the *he/she*, *his/her* options, especially when overused, do tend to end up sounding like the stuffy and rather distant language of legal documents. A further example of the plural pronoun relating to an individual occurs in (6), where *they* has been used in reference to *someone*. It is perfectly acceptable and standard usage for *they* to refer to indefinite pronouns, even singular ones.

Plural indefinite pronouns such as *Everyone, everything* and *everybody* will take a singular verb as they are considered terms with a collective connotation. That said, they clearly refer to more than one person or thing, and this is acknowledged by the later use of *them/their* as seen in (8) and (9).

Everyone in attendance was hoping to receive an apology, but it was not offered to them. (8)

Everybody was using their equipment in low power mode. (9)

Some resources on English grammar do consider (9) to be an informal style and that *Everybody was using his/her* . . . is more acceptable. Again, this seems a little too prescriptive and not a representation of how people speak and write, especially nowadays. The guidance would be even more questionable if applied to (8) and *everyone* was, say, male.

*Everyone in attendance was hoping to receive an apology but it was not offered to him.

In essence, the syntax (see **Glossary**) for these indefinite pronouns is singular (*everyone* taking the singular verb form *was*) but, semantically, there is a clear plural reference (*everyone . . . them*).

A descriptive approach to this makes more sense. For instance, which of the following versions are you more likely to say or hear?

Has everyone got *his/her* passports? †   (10i)

Has everyone got *their* passports? †   (10ii)

And another thing . . . 11

Some reference books suggest that one way around this problem is to use a plural noun.

A tutor is expected to submit his/her lesson plans weekly.

Tutors are expected to submit their lesson plans weekly.

But this advice cannot always be heeded. For a specific instance in which the circumstances indicate an individual (who is not named and whose gender is unimportant), a plural noun change would be unavailable.

The officer leading this case will certainly have their skills tested.

(*Officers leading this case . . .)

The driver of the car has now changed their mind and turns back.

(*Drivers of the car . . .)

12
A specifically indefinite reference

To determine whether a noun requires a definite article, an indefinite article or no article, the reference must first be evaluated for definiteness. This evaluation often depends on the information the writer wishes to express through their writing and the information available to the reader to interpret the writer's words. Essentially, if the writer considers the noun to be a unique instance from the context of the sentence (i.e. the surrounding words), and if the reader will be aware of the exact thing being described, then the reference is definite and the noun can take a definite article.

One way a noun can have a definite reading is if it has already been mentioned (see **13**). A second way is if the writer knows that the reader will already have knowledge of the noun in that particular situation because it is logical and known in everyday life.

> *A research study in the 1980s looked at this problem from a social*
> *perspective. The researcher's findings are listed in the table below.* (1)

Now, the researcher had not been mentioned, but the reader should be aware that a research study is carried out by a researcher. The writer therefore uses a definite article in (1) because the reader knows which researcher is being referred to (the one who carried out the research study). The reader can make the association between the two nouns (*research* and *researcher*).

The reader can also be made aware of the definiteness of the reference if the phrase following it creates a direct association based on the physical surroundings. That is why in (2), *interviewees* is preceded by a definite article because of the prepositional phrase providing the necessary information.

> *The interviewees in the waiting room looked quite nervous, so I went in*
> *and introduced myself.* (2)

Similarly, a definite sense can be inferred in (3) because the reader will again understand the context. The reader will know that the clock being referred to is in the room where the presentation took place.

*After we finished the presentation, we looked at <u>the clock</u> and realised
we had spoken for over 25 minutes.* (3)

The writer can also use a definite article when referring to somebody or something that there can only be one of, owing to the structure of a society or general conventions or practices.

*With demand for reform of the health services, this is a difficult time for
<u>the president.</u>* (There is only one president of a country.) (4)

Unfortunately, <u>the world</u> is still not a safe place for many. (There is only
one world we commonly refer to—our own.) (5)

—Interestingly, definiteness can exist when a singular noun represents its type in a generic sense. The noun stands as an example (like a prototype) with the writer making a general statement about the type.

*<u>The teacher</u> is expected to control the pupils and complete the learning
objectives.* (6)

In (6), *the teacher* is being used to represent all teachers. The writer is not referring to a specific teacher.

◆ ◆ ◆

(7) There are several companies involved and, in fact, a company in the UK is currently researching this material for suitable properties.

(8) It is important that we take time to find the right candidate.

Student enquiry: After reading about definiteness and English articles, wouldn't the definite article be more appropriate than the indefinite in (7) because it is a specific company? And I would have assumed that the noun phrase in (8), *right candidate*, would take an indefinite article because it is not an identifiable person. Surely, if neither the writer nor the reader can identify the specific individual, then it must be indefinite and take *a/an*.

Explanation

Specific and generic are clearly distinct terms. But when applied to article use, this distinction does not neatly translate into specific = a definite reference and generic = an indefinite reference. Something can be specific and indefinite as (7) demonstrates. *A company in the UK* is specific, but it is not definite because the reader is not aware of the company the writer is referring to. The writer does have a particular company in mind, though, so it is considered a specific reference.

It is also possible for a specific reference to take a zero article and not an indefinite one. This happens when the noun is plural. Example (9) describes an event that has taken place: several companies investing in France.

We have seen this in France where <u>companies</u> *have been investing heavily.*   (9)

Because the identity of the companies and the precise number is unknown, or not important, a zero article is used—yet they are still specific companies! Identifying that the noun is specific is not as important as assessing whether the reader will be aware of the exact entity or individual the writer is referring to. That is when we use a definite article, not because the noun reference is specific rather than generic in nature.

In these next examples, we can see specific instances taking different articles.

Specific + definite = *Fifty French students responded to* <u>the survey</u>.   (10)

Specific + indefinite = *My appointment was with* <u>a senior manager</u>
from the corporate office.   (11)

So, when specific instances occur in indefinite situations, they may be called non-unique, which means that the nouns refer to particular individuals or things, but the reader at the time will be unaware of the actual people or things being discussed (or perhaps the writer could create definite awareness but chooses not to, as the reader does not need to know). In (11), the writer may move on to the next topic without revealing the identity of the senior manager. This instance of *manager* is not definite because the writer merely wants the reader to be aware that a meeting took place with a person with that job title.

(8) provides an example of a writer using the definite article (*the right candidate*) even though the person is unknown and therefore not identifiable. This is also evident in (12).

In this situation, the teacher must ensure that <u>the individual</u> *responsible
is not allowed to disrupt the lesson further.*   (12)

Now, the context of the sentence will tell the reader that *the individual* being mentioned is the one who was responsible for the disruption to the lesson, hence the definite article, despite not being identifiable. Likewise, the *right candidate* in (8) will be the individual who is eventually chosen for the role. So, the definiteness here comes not from any known person, but that the company will eventually employ a candidate to fill the position—and presumably the 'right' one.

And another thing . . . 12

Contrary to what might be expected, the definite article is rarely used for providing definitions. When countable nouns are being defined in their singular form they will be preceded by an indefinite article.

An SME can be defined as a company with no more than 50 employees.

*The SME can be defined as . . .

And when an uncountable noun is being defined, it will take a zero article (as will a plural noun).

Brand loyalty is the consumer's commitment to repurchasing a product from the company.

*The brand loyalty is . . .

13

This rule requires a second mention

As discussed in **12**, for a noun to be definite the reader needs to be aware of the exact thing the writer is referring to.

> *My first interviews took place at a school called Cherry Hill Academy.*
> *I arrived at the school at nine o'clock and was ready to conduct the*
> *interviews by ten.* (1)

The second instance of the noun *school* is definite in (1) because the writer has already introduced the institution (*Cherry Hill*), so the reader knows the school the author is referring to. This is known as the second mention rule. Similarly, here in (2) the first mention of the noun is indefinite because the man has yet to be identified, so it is preceded by an indefinite article. In the second instance, the reference is now an identifiable one (or there is at least an awareness of it) and so the noun takes *the*.

> *I saw a man in the lobby of the hotel. The man was carrying a briefcase.* (2)

◆ ◆ ◆

(3) The problem with these markets is that they will continue to suffer long after the economy improves. Indeed, this is a problem that has led some commentators to believe that a different strategy is required.

Student enquiry: I learnt the second mention rule at school for which article to use when. If you mention something in the first instance you use *a* because the reader will not know the thing or person you are talking about. Then, when you mention it/them again, you use *the*. But in (3) the opposite is occurring: the noun takes a definite article (*The problem*) and then an indefinite article (*a problem*) on the second mention. Why is this?

Explanation

Most texts and conversations will move back and forth between generalisations and specific references. Because of this, guidelines such as the first mention/

second mention rule are misleading and unreliable. Each noun instance should be judged on merit, taking into consideration definiteness and countability. There will therefore be occasions when a noun being mentioned for the second time does not take *the* and a noun being mentioned for the first time does. In (3), the initial mention is a unique reference because the writer is implying there is one problem or at least emphasising this particular problem (*the problem*); the second mention, although relating to the first, is more a general point about problems of this type and so the noun takes an indefinite article. Consider this example.

> *The loyalty of customers in this industry has not been studied in great detail. One study has shown, however, loyalty in the insurance industry can be affected by bad reputation and a disjointed value chain.* (4)

In (4), although it is being mentioned a second time and has additional information restricting the reference (. . . *in the insurance industry*), the uncountable noun *loyalty* does not require an article in the second sentence: the reference is indefinite because it is relating to a concept in general terms. This may come as a surprise given that both instances are referring to particular types of loyalty— that of customers in the insurance industry. But it is the *of*-phrase that allows a definite article to be used initially (no article is also possible in this first instance). And had the writer selected the compound *customer loyalty* instead, a definite article would not have been necessary.

Other scenarios in which a definite article can be employed for a first mention include when the noun is in the immediate situation or the physical surroundings. Logic might also allow the reader to have awareness of a noun's definiteness without it having been previously introduced (see **12**). Equally, the second mention may not refer to the original noun. The rule is also redundant when the first mention is a generic reference relating to type and the second mention is a specific person but not one that requires identifying (5).

> *Unfortunately, the supervisor is never around when you need them. But a supervisor did finally arrive the following day and I was able to finish.* (5)

And another thing . . . 13

In fiction writing, a definite article is sometimes employed stylistically to make it feel as though the reader is joining events halfway through—thus putting them closer to the action. The report in this next example has not been mentioned before; in fact, this is the opening line of the story.

> *The report had been read maybe a dozen times, but the sequence of events was no clearer in the minds of those who had gathered for the hearing.*

14

Are some proper nouns more definite than others?

A proper noun differs from a common noun in that it states the actual name of a person or thing (see 1). And although they have a definite sense, proper nouns are not preceded by an article.

| *I would like to thank Mark Jones for his three years of support.* | (1) |

| *This has also occurred on several occasions in Japan.* | (2) |

However, proper nouns do take a definite article if *the* is considered part of their name or common usage has led them to take *the*.

| *I will now compare the stock markets of the UK and Hong Kong.* | (3) |

| *They have already mapped a quarter of the Atlantic Ocean.* | (4) |

| *She'd always wanted to work for the BBC.* | (5) |

Interestingly, proper nouns can also occur with definite articles if there is an adjective modifying the noun.

| *The well-dressed Mr Hanson walked confidently into the meeting.* | (6) |

◆ ◆ ◆

(7) This is not a Governor Reynolds that I am familiar with.†

(8) A Mr Andrews enquired about you last week.†

Student enquiry: It would be helpful to understand why the names of the people in (7) and (8) occur with indefinite articles when, as proper nouns, they should be taking zero articles.

Explanation

We have already seen that some proper nouns can take definite articles. But here we have two situations in which indefinite articles have been employed. The first point to make is that the source is more likely to be spoken English than an example of academic writing. In (7), the speaker is referring to the way the governor has acted in a certain situation. The governor's actions have surprised the speaker, so they have used the indefinite article to, in effect, split the governor's character into two—the governor that the speaker knows and the governor that has acted in this particular way (actually, the speaker could also have chosen the definite article to achieve the same effect *This is not the Governor Reynolds that . . .*). This practice can also be adopted for places.

> The California *I know would never allow these disasters to affect morale.*   (9)

In reality, most names are not unique and people can share the same title. This is why in (8), as the speaker is not familiar with Mr Andrews (i.e. does not know him) they use the indefinite article instead of the zero article to indicate this. Compare conversations (10i) and (10ii). Assuming the recipient does not know the gentleman, the use of an indefinite article (10i) will probably produce a simple rhetorical response because the statement is set up to indicate that the person may be unknown to them. The use of a zero article (10ii) will likely lead to a query about who this person is and extend the length of the exchange.

> *A Mr Andrews enquired about you last week.*†   *Oh, OK.*†   (10i)

> *Mr Andrews enquired about you last week.*†   *Who?* †   (10ii)

And another thing . . . 14

Proper nouns may take a definite article if confirmation is required about the identity of something or someone.

> *I am talking about* the King George *who married Princess Caroline.*†

In this next example, the speaker is clarifying that an individual is not the famous person that shares his name. Stress would be placed on the definite article if spoken (pronounced *thee*). Note the use of both indefinite and definite articles here.

> *There is* a *Michael Douglas on the staff, but it is not* the *Michael Douglas.*†

15
Can't we just omit articles?

Articles in English assist the reader or listener in identifying and following the relationship between the nouns and the other elements of the sentence. A noun or noun phrase is likely to require an article unless it is a proper noun, a fixed phrase or an uncountable or plural noun being used in an indefinite way. If the reference is considered definite (see **12**), then the noun will take a definite article regardless of countability. Those of the opinion that articles are optional or needless, as meaning can be inferred without them, might care to assess the quality of the following extract with the articles omitted.

> *Report from leading trade magazine states that growth in sector, which is always largest sector of developed country, nearly ground to halt in first month of year. Picture is not pretty one. Optimism is lot weaker than year ago. I visited region recently and interviewed man who spoke out against government. His company was one that refused to agree to recent sanctions. Manager of medium-sized firm began by telling me that employees are little fazed by situation at moment. Firm, located on east coast, has had issue with dwindling labour pool as well.* (1)

There are a couple of considerations here. The first involves style. It sounds as though it has been written by someone with a weak grasp of the language. The sentences seem cropped and feel disconnected. The second is semantic, i.e. the relation between the words and their intended reference. There are ambiguous noun phrases throughout, where the reader is unable to follow either meaning or reference. The following excerpts will demonstrate this:

> *. . . and interviewed man who spoke out against government.*

Here, we do not know whether it was *the man* who made headlines for being the only one to speak out against the government or *a man*, one of perhaps several who have spoken out against the government in recent weeks. Either way, this countable noun does require an article.

> *His company was one that refused to agree to recent sanctions.*

The reader interprets the zero article before *one* to mean one of a few who have refused the sanctions. But as the writer is not using articles, they may have meant *the one* company that refused the sanctions, i.e. all the other companies complied with the sanctions.

> ... *employees are little fazed by situation at moment.*

Article selection is crucial here because no article (*little fazed*) means the employees are not discouraged or deterred by the situation, whereas an indefinite article (*a little fazed*) means they are upset and discouraged by the situation (see also **39**).

> *Firm, located on east coast ...*

Here, a zero article is not appropriate. The reader does not know whether this is referring to the firm mentioned earlier (*The firm*) or a different one (*A firm*). A definite article will inform the reader that the original firm is located on the east coast; an indefinite article that it is not.

What these instances show is that omitting articles is not merely a stylistic device but a practice that heavily affects understanding and interpretation.

◆ ◆ ◆

(2) She became ambassador for the islands in 1998.

(3) Subjects were observed for twenty minutes and target regions were identified.

Student enquiry: As a country or region tends to have only one *ambassador*, I would expect the noun in (2) to have a definite article. For instance, we say *this is a difficult time for the president* because there can be only one president. And in (3), I am unsure why there is no definite article at the start. The *subjects* must have been introduced by this point or they can at least be inferred by the reader, so isn't it a definite reference and therefore should take a definite article?

Explanation

The definite article can sometimes be omitted when a noun is referring to a person in an institutional role. But this can only occur when the noun or noun phrase functions as a subject complement (2), not when it is the object of the sentence (4).

> *I managed to speak to the ambassador.*   (4)

> **I managed to speak to ambassador.*

(3) is an example of a writer of science looking to present a method or process as concisely as possible to communicate to the reader the general steps. To achieve this, the writer decides to omit the definite articles despite the reader being aware

of the reference. This is more likely to be a practice employed for plural nouns, but the writer does run the risk of ambiguity when omitting articles in this fashion (see earlier discussion).

And another thing . . . 15

Journalists are likely to be restricted by word count and space in their assignments and so require a concise style of writing. Articles are often the first words to be removed, especially from newspaper headlines.

Employee earns record payout after three years
of abuse from manager

Articles are often removed from chapter headings, as seen in this academic paper.

CONTENTS:

And, ordinarily, this figure label would have at least three articles.

Figure 4.3 Comparison of scores between groups for first six questions

Understanding 1–15

Note: some questions may have more than one correct answer. Some questions may have no correct or no incorrect answers.

1. A. Which one of these nouns might take a capital letter despite not being a proper noun?

   distance   change   beauty

   B. Which of the following should have an initial capital letter?

   shakespearian   infrastructure   lawyer   indian   government

2. A. Which of these uncountable nouns can be subdivided or split up without the need for a partitive phrase?

   advice   information   ability

   B. Which of the following descriptions applies to uncountable nouns?

   unbounded   cannot be used with a definite article

   cannot be used with *much*   cannot take on a partitive phrase

3. A. Which of the following terms can be collectivised?

   partridge   monkey   sugar

   B. Which of these can take a plural verb (e.g. are, were)?

   10,000 pounds   10,000 hours

   10,000 people   10,000 kilometres

4. A. Which of the following is NOT a collective noun?

   committee   board   people

   B. Which of these sentences could take a plural verb?

   The board is meeting today.   The board is split on this issue.

   The board is dominated by male members.

5. A. The first word of which of these compounds can be made plural?

child support   system analyst   insect spray

B. Which of these statements is true?

When two words in a compound have equal weight, they will be hyphen-ated.

Only irregular plurals can act as the modifier in a compound.

In compound adjectives the stress will fall on the second part.

6. A. Which of these genitive forms is correctly written?

childrens' activities   June's month   the bus's engine

B. Which of these statements about *of*-phrases is false?

They are usually associated with new information.

They are usually informal in tone.

They often contain impersonal references.

7. A. Which of these phrases shows the correct order of words?

too small a target   too small target   a too small target

B. Which of the following cannot appear before a definite article?

more   much   most

8. A. Which of these uses of *some* is for emphasis?

Some lesson was on.   There was some lesson in there.

That was some lesson.

B. What type of noun cannot be used with the determiner *any*?

singular   plural   uncountable   All three types can be used.

9. A. Which of these phrases will require a plural verb form?

The petition and later demonstration   The hallway and lounge

The captain and leader

B. Which of these is least likely to be an approximation?

5 or 6   7 or 9   20 or 30   50 or 55

10. A. Which of these instances of *we* has a generic connotation?

We left a lot before that.   We are conditioned to that.

We are nervous, though.

B. Which of the following instances of *we* is equivalent in meaning to 'you'?

We do have confidence today.   We can do that, can we?

We will meet them in a coffee shop.

11. A. In which construction could *they* refer to an individual?

They drive to work.   They meet on Tuesdays.   They work together.

B. Which of these pronouns should be used to fill in the gap?

In the men's tournament a golfer used ____ putter to escape the hazard.

its   his   her   their

12. A. What articles are appropriate for a specific reference?

zero and indefinite articles   definite article   all three

B. Which of these sentences is clearly referring to a specific company?

The company should do that for them.

A company changes its mind at stage three.

A large company chooses this option rather than withdrawing.

13. A. What is the correct order for articles in a paragraph?

There is no set order.   zero, indefinite then definite

indefinite then definite

B. What reasons might allow a writer to use a definite article for the first mention of a noun?

the immediate situation or surroundings

a logical relationship with something else

a wish to create urgency

14. A. In which instance might you NOT use an article before a person's name?

when discussing a stranger

when the listener knows the individual

for clarifying someone's identity

B. There are two Mr Andrews in a company, and they work in different departments. Both of them are well known in the company. Which of the following forms would NOT be likely for one colleague to say to another?

Mr Andrews from accounts called.   A Mr Andrews from accounts called.

The Mr Andrews from accounts called.

15. A. In which situation(s) might a writer remove all the articles?

   In a headline   In a title   In a scientific description

   B. Which of these contains incorrect article use?

   The president is unavailable.   He was president for ten years.

   President visited last year.   The country changed president recently.

B. VERBS (TENSE, MOOD, AND MODALS)

16

Conversion: When words switch classes

English is a fluid language that is constantly evolving. New words are created and old ones manipulated all the time. One method of creating words is through conversion. Conversion occurs when an existing word is adopted by or utilised in a different word class.

When a verb has originated from a noun, the verb often relates to an action that is based on a typical characteristic of the noun.

noun—*hare* (animal)   verb—*to hare (about)*

noun—*water* (substance)   verb—*to water (the plants)*

An interesting conversion is the noun *pocket*, which in its converted verb form concerns the action of putting something into a pocket.

> He <u>pocketed</u> the change quickly.   (1)

Another noun that has experienced conversion is *ship*. In truth, when something is shipped it does not necessarily mean transported by ship.

> They will be <u>shipped</u> tomorrow to the address provided along with
> the other products.   (2)

And a recent example of converting a noun into a verb is *to Google*, from the act of using the search engine of the same name.

> I use <u>Google</u> when I want to find out about something. (noun)   (3i)

> Did you <u>Google</u> it? † (verb)   (3ii)

—Correspondingly, when a noun is formed from a verb using this process, it will often relate to the outcome of the action.

verb—to drive   noun—a drive

So, the action of driving results in *a drive* in a car.

◆   ◆   ◆

(4) The build has gone well so far.

(5) We could contract these further to make it easier.

(6) The wise have no time for these matters.

Student enquiry: Is it OK to use the verb *to build* like a noun, as occurs in (4)? And in (5), this use of *contract* as a verb does not seem to relate at all to the noun *contract*, which is an agreement between two people. Also, would (6) be regarded as an instance of conversion because *wise* is usually an adjective but seems to be a noun here?

Explanation

The outcome of building a house is the house itself: the noun is a derivation of the verb *to build*. So, (4) is an example of conversion. The two terms have related meanings and are said to be polysemes (see **Glossary**). Here is a further example.

There are a lot of new builds in this area. (7)

It also seems as though conversion may have taken place in (5); however, the noun *contract* and the verb *contract* have unrelated meanings. (5) is not an example of conversion; these are just two independent words with the same spelling. And instead of being polysemes they are referred to as homonyms (see **Glossary**).

contract (noun)—an agreement between two or more parties

contract (verb)—to reduce in size; to shrink

Semantic shifts can lead to two words that were at one time polysemes reduced to simply homonyms. This means words that were historically connected are now no longer related in meaning; yet some homonyms may have never had a natural link to each other.

When spoken, identical verb and noun forms can be distinguished. The stress on the noun will fall on a different part of the word from the verb.

noun—próduce   verb—to prodúce

In the verb form above there is a slight pause between the *pro-* and the *-duce*, which is not necessary when pronouncing the noun form.

Here are some more examples. Note where the accent falls.

noun	cómpound	cóntract	éxtract	récord
verb	compóund	contráct	extráct	recórd

—Some adjectives can be converted to, or at least take on the appearance of, nouns. With the addition of a definite article they are equivalent to 'those who are (adjective).' We have an example of this in (6). But the conversion is not absolute because these terms are still modified by adverbs (8) and cannot take a possessive case (9).

I would categorise them as the very wise. (8)

*The wise's way is to question everything. (9)

Sometimes they refer to a specific group rather than a general type.

The guilty were taken out of the courthouse. (10)

And another thing . . . 16

Reference books can be a source of confusion where polysemes (see **Glossary**) and homonyms are concerned. Some dictionaries focus simply on the spelling of the word and thus contain a single entry with multiple items regardless of the semantic relationship. Here is a dictionary entry for the term *contract*.

Contract—(*noun*) a written or spoken agreement enforceable by law

(*verb*) decrease in size, number or range

There is an argument for two separate entries here because the instances are distinct (unrelated). And this format would perhaps be more helpful to the learner of English.

Contract—(*noun*) a written or spoken agreement enforceable by law

Contract—(*verb*) decrease in size, number or range

Compare this now with the term *produce*. The two definitions are related, so a single dictionary entry is appropriate.

Produce—(*verb*) make or manufacture from components or raw materials

(*noun*) agricultural and other natural products collectively

It would surely make sense for homonyms to occur as multiple entries and polysemes to come under a single entry. That said, it can be difficult to tell whether two words are true homonyms. Words derived from foreign terms or that have experienced a shift or corruption in meaning could provide a test to those researching their origins and trying to implement this advice.

17
The missing object of the transitive

A verb can be classified in several ways. One category is the distinction between transitive and intransitive and this relates to sentence structure. Transitive verbs are said to express an action. They are also said to require an object, which will be a noun phrase.

They _love_ this scheme.† (1)

Verbs that are used intransitively do not take objects.

Yes, we _talk_.† (2)

Many verbs, though, can be employed both transitively (3i, 4i) and intransitively (3ii, 4ii). Note that there is often a difference in meaning between the two forms.

Michael _changed_ companies again.† (3i)

I was not the only one to think Michael _changed_. (3ii)

We have _left_ this second issue for later. (4i)

No, she has also _left_.† (4ii)

The transitive instance in (3i) reports Michael moving to another company. The intransitive form refers to a difference in Michael's character. The transitive in (4i) tells us something has been put on hold or set aside for later. The intransitive (4ii) refers to an absence or departure.

◆ ◆ ◆

(5) I will respond with an email.†

(6) I was thankful that Ken agreed to edit.

Student enquiry: I looked up the verbs _respond_ and _edit_ in the dictionary and it said they were intransitive and transitive respectively. Why, then, does _respond_ have an object in (5) when it shouldn't have one and _edit_ has no object attached to it in (6) when it requires one?

Explanation

The intransitive verb *respond* does not have an object in (5); it is just a prepositional phrase that is adding extra information. The presence of an infinitive phrase may also give this impression, i.e. that an intransitive is taking an object.

They arrived to see that the event had already begun.   (7)

Edit in (6) is indeed a transitive verb, but the writer has used ellipsis (see **Glossary**) and omitted the object (*it/the document*). Leaving the object out is especially common when its identity is clear from the context.

Jane writes as well.†   (8)

It is also a well-established practice for a transitive verb to be used intransitively for a habitual or general action (as opposed to a specific occurrence of that action).

Yes, we give at Thanksgiving too.†   *It's not often that I refuse.*   (9, 10)

In fact, there are very few verbs that must, in all instances, occur with a clear direct object present. The writer in (11) has used transitive verbs without needing to include objects for them.

He often takes but rarely gives during these sessions.   (11)

And in conditional *if*-sentences a transitive verb may not require an object either.

If you like, we can change it.†   (12)

Here we have a passive construction with a transitive verb lacking a direct object.

The issue has been discussed.   (13)

Looking at this in reverse, we can see that it is not possible for intransitive verbs (here, *arrive* and *go*) to take direct objects.

*We arrive the airport in the evening.   **I will go the office soon.*

And another thing . . . 17

Most verbs, then, cannot be pinned down to one category or one meaning. And the common definition that verbs are 'doing' words that denote an action and are modified by adverbs is not always accurate either. In this next example, the first instance of the verb relates to an action but the second to a state. It follows that the meaning of the verb will be different for each instance.

I see the manager in half an hour.†

I see you've changed the format again.†

Linking or copular verbs will also relate to a state and not an action. And they take subject complements, not objects.

She <u>seemed</u> confused by the change of venue.

So, not all instances of verbs denote action. But even ones that do might not be modified by adverbs. Here, an action verb appears alongside a complement headed by an adjective.

I <u>arrived</u> worried and unable to concentrate (see also **34**).

18
The verb with various forms

We can divide verbs into five standard forms: the infinitive, the present tense (simple), the past tense (simple), the past participle and the present participle. The only differences between the simple present and the infinitive form are that *to* occurs in the latter, and the former can be inflected (by adding an *s*). The following selection of regular (R) and irregular (IR) verbs will demonstrate these standard forms.

	INFINITIVE	PRESENT	PAST	PAST PARTICIPLE	PRESENT PARTICIPLE
(R)	to announce	announce(s)	announced	announced	announcing
(R)	to complete	complete(s)	completed	completed	completing
(R)	to request	request(s)	requested	requested	requesting
(IR)	to rise	rise(s)	rose	risen	rising
(IR)	to spend	spend(s)	spent	spent	spending
(IR)	to write	write(s)	wrote	written	writing

Note: The infinitive form without the *to* is known as the base form or bare infinitive.

A quick examination reveals that the past tense and past participles of regular verbs are identical and end in *-ed*. For the irregular verbs shown, none of the forms end in *-ed* and some of them have different past participles from their past forms. However, there is no variation in the present participles and all end in *-ing* whether derived from regular or irregular verbs.

—Some verbs have both regular and irregular types. When *to cost* has the meaning of to calculate or estimate the future price of something, it is transitive and regular in form.

We <u>costed</u> the materials required for the visits. (simple past) (1)

But when the verb means 'how much money is required to buy something', then it has an irregular form with no difference between its base form and its past tense.

It cost us a lot of money in the end. (simple past)   (2)

◆ ◆ ◆

(3) Which verb(s) do these forms belong to?

been/am/were/are/is

Student enquiry: I saw this question (3) in an English language learning book. Now, I know that *been* and *is* are forms of the verb *to be*, but I am not sure about the others. I want to say that *were* is a modal but I'm not certain. *Am* and *are* must be the same verb. In fact, I think *are* may be a form of *be* as well.

Explanation

They are all forms of the verb *to be*. Unlike other verbs, *be* uses three forms for its present tense: one for the first person singular, another for the second person singular and still another for the third person singular. To add to the confusion, they bear no resemblance to the verb's base or dictionary form. Compare the verb with another irregular verb, *to rise*.

INFINITIVE	PRESENT	PAST	PAST PARTICIPLE	PRESENT PARTICIPLE
to rise	rise(s)	rose	risen	rising
to be	am, is, are	was, were	been	being

Even though *rise* is irregular and has a past form of *rose* and a different form for its past participle, these only represent an internal vowel change and inflection, and all its forms are comparable to the base form. We have already mentioned *be* has three simple present forms that are distinct from the base form. We can also see it has two simple past forms that are again unrelated in spelling to the simple present. The participles, however, do show some relation to the root.

Two more points of interest: the past tense form (*was*) can combine with *to* to give the meaning of *would*, describing an eventual action.

The town square was to become a symbol of this peaceful revolution.   (4)

The verb also has an action form, where it takes on the meaning of behave.

Make sure you be good today; no arguing with the teachers, ok? †   (5)

And another thing . . . 18

Perhaps an even more exceptional verb is *beware*, which has no tense forms or participles and is used only for requests, warnings or instructions (such as *beware of falling rocks*) and in the infinitive (*I told them to beware of falling rocks*).

This defective verb can also be used in a theatrical or stylistic way immediately before a noun phrase.

Beware the strange inhabitants of the moor.

19
Doubling up on regular verb forms

There are no fixed rules or system for the way irregular verbs are spelled in their various forms. For regular verbs, there are some set patterns. When forming the past tense, if the word ends in *y* and is preceded by a consonant, the *y* is replaced with an *i* before *-ed* is added.

> *We <u>studied</u> this species in its natural environment.* (study)   (1)

When a word ends consonant-vowel-consonant and is one syllable in length, the final consonant is doubled before it is inflected.

> *We <u>tripped</u> up on this last equation.* (trip)   (2)

—For the present participle, if the word ends in *y* then *-ing* is added.

> *She is <u>carrying</u> this team at the moment.* (carry)   (3)

When the word ends in *ie* it is replaced with *y* before *-ing* is added.

> *It seems they were <u>lying</u> about this final incident.* (lie)   (4)

If the word is more than one syllable in length, then the final consonant is only doubled if the stress falls on the final syllable.

> *This is <u>happening</u> in the next few weeks.* (<u>hap</u>pen)   (5)

> *I am <u>beginning</u> to realise that further efforts will be required.* (be<u>gin</u>)   (6)

◆ ◆ ◆

(7) They eventually paid the money.

(8) This was key to focusing on the task at hand.

(9) Several of the students were panicked by these events.

(10) I will be travelling in a few weeks.

Student enquiry: I have the following observations about these four examples in light of the standard rules for the spelling of regular verbs:

(7) This should be *paied* according to the rules, but this is obviously incorrect.

(8) I would have expected the *s* to double to create *focussing*.

(9) Why is there the addition of a *k* here?

(10) Surely the stress is on the initial syllable which means the consonant should not be doubled, leaving *traveling*?

Explanation

(7) As the consonant is preceded by a vowel, the rule does not apply. When *y* is preceded by *a* (as in *lay, repay, say, pay*) it ends in *id* not *ied*.

(8) In this example the stress on the verb *focus* does fall on the second syllable. But usage can vary between one consonant and two when an *s* follows a vowel. This is also true of *bias/biased/biassed*.

(9) A *k* is added after the final *c* in some words (*picnicking, trafficking*).

(10) In BrE, the letter *l* is doubled regardless of the applied stress.

In AmE (11, 12) the letter *l* is not doubled when it comes after a soft vowel.

> *This has now been <u>canceled</u>.*   (11)

> *We have <u>labeled</u> these 'amendments'.*   (12)

And another thing . . . 19

BrE also breaks the 'doubling' rule for the following terms with unstressed final syllables ending in *m* and *p*.

> program—*They will have to reassess their <u>programming</u> protocols.*

> worship—*<u>Worshipping</u> of this piece of land is a recent custom.*

But other words ending in *p* retain the single consonant.

> *We have been <u>developing</u> a method to reintroduce this product.*

20
A present reading of a past action

A verb phrase in the simple past tense may give no indication about when the action occurred or how long it lasted. It may simply express that the action was in the past and has now been completed. Of course, the timing may be revealed by a time expression.

> *We changed our method last week.* (1)

But we cannot assume that the circumstances of the past action remain the same at the time of writing or at the time of the utterance, i.e. that the action occurred in the past and does not occur now. The simple past tense merely relates to something that happened at a point in time or a state that existed.

> *Actually, Michael lived in Japan when we went there.*† (2)

Michael may still live in Japan, but the past tense is used because he lived there at the time they visited. (2) could be a response to the suggestion that Michael had not yet moved to Japan at that point. They might also have responded using the past progressive (*Michael was living . . .*).

—Interestingly, the past tense can be used for an enquiry that is occurring in the present. It has the effect of adding a layer of politeness. In the following examples, the present tense (3) conveys a more direct and stronger emotion than the less assertive past does (4).

> *Excuse me, I want to know why these are not in the sale?* † (3)

> *Excuse me, I wanted to know why these are not in the sale?* † (4)

◆ ◆ ◆

(5) Well, I was in the office when this research student walks in and asks about my project.†

(6) Lord Thomson storms out of meeting.

(7) Manev uses both poetic and prose renditions in this piece.

(8) Grace says that you left last week; is that true?†

Student enquiry: I am surprised at the mixing of tenses and time in these examples. In (5), the action happened in the past but the writer is using the present form (*walks*). Similarly, for (6), why is the present tense (*storms out*) used when the action is clearly in the past? (7) contains another present tense form this time for a historical work. In (8), a past action is being discussed and there is further use of a present form (*says*).

Explanation

In (5), the writer is using what is known as the historic present. It is a form of narration that serves to bring the reader closer to the action or event. It then appears as if the writer is returning to the past to narrate events as they unfold.

It is likely that (6) is a headline. The writer is trying to catch the attention of the reader and the present tense does this more effectively than the past does. Again, when events appear to be unfolding at the present time they have more immediacy and are more vivid. That is why newspaper editors adopt the tense to produce eye-catching headlines.

The writer in (7) is adopting a device in which the present tense can refer to the work, specifically the method or style, of a famous person (even if they are dead) because their output is considered to be fixed in the present, i.e. when the work is being viewed, read or listened to—or perhaps even because their work is seen as timeless!

In (8), the person is seeking confirmation about something Grace said. The focus here is not on the timing of when Grace said this but on whether the utterance was true. The communication, in all probability, would needed to have taken place recently (see also **23**). This particular use of the present tense is limited to certain verbs like *say, tell* and *hear*.

> Harry <u>tells</u> me you have fixed the machine.   (9)

> I <u>hear</u> you visited the gallery last week.   (10)

And another thing . . . 20

Sometimes it is difficult to know what tense the verb form is in.

> I <u>put</u> the ingredients in the bowl.

This is known as syncretism (see **Glossary**). An example of it is an irregular verb having the same form for the past and present tense (see also *shut* below). Naturally, it can result in ambiguity between a past and present reading; often though, the context or the words associating with the verb will indicate what tense it is.

I <u>put</u> the ingredients in the bowl and then <u>stir</u>.

In the example above, another verb in the sentence (*stir*) informs us the initial verb is in the present tense. And here, the time references provide the necessary information.

I <u>shut</u> the gate in the evening. (present)

I <u>shut</u> the gate yesterday.   (past)

21
Presenting the future in the past

There are no inflected verb forms when discussing future time in English. Instead, we can use the modals *will* or *shall*.

> *We will develop this model over the next six months.* (1)

But when there is a future time expression in the sentence, there may be no need for these modal verbs.

> *We visit these ruins on <u>the final day</u> of our trip.* (2)

In (2), the action has been planned or fixed to the extent that a present tense form can be employed. Clearly, then, *will* is not always required for expressing future time. In fact, *will* has many other uses that are unrelated to future reference. Verbs as well as nouns and adjectives can also be used to discuss future events. This all serves to illustrate that English cannot be considered as having any meaningful future tense.

◆ ◆ ◆

(3) When you change the report, upload it to the folder.

(4) The storm hits the mainland in the morning.

(5) I forgot that you began your new job next week.†

Student enquiry: I have identified these three sentences as all referring to the future. Yet (3) and (4) have present tense forms, and the verb in (5) is in the past tense. How can these tenses appear in sentences that discuss the future?

Explanation

Referring to future time in English is not a straightforward process. Oddly enough, quite often the present tense and the past tense are used to refer to events that will take place in the future. In (3), the scenario of the changing of the report is fixed for the purposes of the conversation and so the present can be employed.

This use is common in conditional sentences and in dependent and adverbial clauses. Inserting *will* would be ungrammatical here. The verb is in the simple present form in the main clause in (4) because the action or event is deemed inevitable (at least according to the meteorologists). Perhaps this is a little presumptuous. Usually, present tense for future time is employed in this way when there is certainty that an event will take place.

In (5) we have a past tense form (*began*) being used for future time because the reference is not the starting of the job next week but the fact of forgetting. Again, there is an element of certainty that the event (starting the job) will happen. Interestingly, the present form *begin* would be equally valid here, as would the modal form *will begin*.

And another thing . . . 21

The present tense can be adopted for a future event that is habitual enough (it is known as the habitual present) for the simple present to be available. The assumption is that the action has occurred so frequently in the past and is likely to occur in the future so can take a present reading.

Who will check your research over for mistakes?   Oh, Mauro edits our papers.†

22

The peculiar perfect progressive

The perfect aspect in its present tense form is employed when an action began at some time in the past and has extended up to the present. In other words, it is inclusive of the present or relevant to the present.

You have answered all my questions so are free to leave.† (1)

A more explicit example that effectively contrasts the simple past with the present perfect is this response (2) to the question of whether someone is familiar with a certain vehicle.

They have driven the C23. (2)

Using the simple past here (*They drove the C23*) would also indicate that the person has driven the vehicle at some point but perhaps only once. The present perfect is more effective in answering the question and communicating the notion of familiarity, in this case with a vehicle, because of its inclusive nature.

The past perfect is used for an action in the past that was completed before another action.

*We had observed that species before Morgan and Dewson conducted
their study.* (3)

The future perfect is employed for an action that will be completed at a stated point in the future. In (4), two events are referenced: the sponsors arriving (the time reference) and the sorting of the data (the action or event).

We will have sorted the data by the time the sponsors arrive. (4)

—The progressive aspect is used for an action or event in progress or at least one that has the capability of continuing. Here is the present progressive.

We are looking at several options for reducing the consumption. (5)

The activity does not need to be taking place at that moment for the progressive aspect to be used. In (6), the speaker is referring to an ongoing activity and the stage they have reached in their essay, though they may not be currently engaged in the task. When there is an apparent completion point for the activity, use of the progressive indicates, unsurprisingly, that the action has yet to be completed (7).

I am finishing my method statement.† (6)

I am writing up my research. I hope to have it finished in a few weeks.† (7)

The action may not yet have started. Using the present progressive for a future event indicates the speaker's/writer's confidence that the action will occur though.

We are getting the money when he returns.† (8)

I am revising all day on Monday.† (9)

It is a mistake to think that progressive clauses will always be active in structure.

The images are being fixed. (10)

—These two aspects (perfect and progressive) can be combined when referring to a continuous action that occurred in the past but has some relevance to the present (present perfect progressive, 11), to a continuous action that was completed before another past action began (past perfect progressive, 12) and to a continuous action that will be completed sometime in the future (future perfect progressive, 13).

We have been collecting data on this event. (11)

Well, they had been warning them that this might happen.† (12)

I will have been working there three years this July. (13)

◆ ◆ ◆

(14i) The choice of location was a strange one, but the community room may have been being used at the time.

(15i) It has been being extended for about fifteen years now.

Student enquiry: I do not recognise the tense in either (14i) or (15i). I assume it is some form of the perfect progressive. Also, these sentences do not sound right to me. Are they grammatically correct?

Explanation

These perfect progressive sentences (14i and 15i) look and sound inelegant because they are also passive constructions and contain several auxiliaries in a row. Although they are grammatical, there are often better alternatives.

The choice of location was a strange one, but the community room
may have been in use at the time. (14ii)

They <u>have been</u> extending it for about fifteen years now.   (15ii)

Two caveats to also bear in mind. First, without time expressions these construc-tions (in 14i and 15i) are less justifiable. Second, the duration of the act or event may need to be of sufficient length for the passive perfect progressive to be appropriate. Compare the following:

It has been being developed since yesterday.   (16i)

It has been being developed since 2012.   (16ii)

For (16i), an alternative such as *The development began yesterday* would be better.

And another thing . . . 22

The positions of the auxiliaries and participles are fixed when combined in this way.

is + used

is + being + used

has + been + used

has + been + being + used

may + have + been + being + used

*They have being been a little bit ambitious with this.

*They have might been a little bit ambitious with this.

23

Reporting on backshifting

Speech may be reported directly through a quotation (1i) or by indirectly relaying what a person has said (1ii).

'We lost our main investor,' he admitted. (1i)

He admitted that they had lost their main investor. (1ii)

The quote in (1i) reports exactly what was said by the individual. (1ii) provides the content but not the exact words. Note that the two forms also employ different tenses. The direct reported speech is in the simple past tense and the indirect is in the past perfect. When the direct speech is in the present tense (2i), there is often a switch to the past for indirectly reporting it (2ii).

'There <u>are</u> no errors in the second program,' added the scientist. (2i)

The scientist added that there <u>were</u> no errors in the second program. (2ii)

◆ ◆ ◆

(3) She told me they are discussing this issue.

(4) They didn't know the conference had already taken place.

(5i) Rachel says that the conference starts at 10 a.m.†

Student enquiry: I am assuming that (3) is reporting the direct speech *We are discussing this issue* (she said). So why does the writer choose a present tense instead of using the past tense *She told me they were discussing that issue?* For (4), I can see that this is indirect reported speech, but it is not clear to me what the initial speech act was. And in (5i), again, the verb is in the present tense for an indirect reported speech act that must have taken place in the past.

Explanation

The process of changing from present to past tense and past to past perfect tense in reported speech is known as backshifting. But there may be instances where backshifting need not be applied.

If the topic is still relevant or valid, then there is no cause to backshift the tenses for reporting the speech act. In (3), the issue is still being discussed, so the present tense is appropriate for the second part of the sentence (note, though, that the writer can still choose to use the past form of the reporting verb *tell*). The determiners and pronouns may not change in this instance either; again in (3), *this* is used instead of *that*.

For communication that has occurred recently, the reporting verb may also remain in the present (6) (see also **20**).

> Michael <u>says</u> that you went last week ...†   (6)

In (4), a speech act is not being reported in the way we have seen previously. We can only really guess what the original statement might have been.

Now let's consider a reason why a writer or a speaker might choose to backshift the tenses. Sometimes it is to show that they do not necessarily agree with or believe the statement they are reporting. In (5i) the thing being reported is still taking place or is applicable, and so the present tense is employed with no judgement on Rachel's claim. If the reporter does not agree that the conference starts at 10 a.m., though, then backshifting can express this. Here in (5ii), they are disputing Rachel's claim and adopting the past tense.

> Rachel <u>said</u> that the conference <u>started</u> at 10 a.m. (but it actually starts at 11).†   (5ii)

And another thing . . . 23

When reporting speech, inversion can occur between the speaker and the reporting verb. Here, a choice is available to the writer for the verb *to admit*.

> 'The findings are not conclusive,' admitted the tutor / the tutor admitted.

An exception is the verb *to tell*, which requires an object and so cannot be inverted in this way.

> 'The findings are not conclusive,' the researcher told me.

> *'The findings are not conclusive,' told the researcher.

24
Conditions for conditionals

The dual-clause conditional construction can relate to possible situations (1i), hypothetical situations that are possible (1ii) and events that can no longer take place (1iii).

If I change the title, I can include section four.† (1i)

If I changed the title, I could include section four.† (1ii)

If I had changed the title, I could have included section four. (1iii)

Note the underlined tense changes in the two clauses in the set of examples (1). The choice of conditional will depend on how confident the writer is that the event takes place.

—There is also a general truth or 'zero' conditional (2i) which relates to a habitual action and outcome.

When I finish a section, I save the file.† (2i)

The inference in (2) is that when(ever) they finish a section, they (always) save the file.

—The main clause can just as easily come first.

I save the file when I finish a section.† (2ii)

Either of the clauses in a conditional can be negative (3), or they can both be (4).

She wouldn't have lost the case if she had read those documents. (3)

If I hadn't have emailed them, I wouldn't have known about the meeting.† (4)

—To create a more formal style, and perhaps a more tentative reading, *should* can be inserted before the simple present verb form.

If you should lose this information, then you would need to re-register. (5)

Another option here is to omit the *if* and invert the subject and the modal.

Should you lose this information, then you would need to re-register. (6)

❖ ❖ ❖

(7) If I was confrontational, I would have told him to his face.

(8) If they only registered last week, the paperwork will not be ready for a few more days.†

(9) If you saw him, then he was only there for a few minutes.†

Student enquiry: I am interested in the rules governing the different conditional types. My understanding is that for the hypothetical condition when the *if*-clause is past tense, then the main clause contains *would/could*. Yet, in (7) *would have* is used instead. Also, the two clauses in (8) sound strange, as though the tenses do not match. In (9), both clauses are simple past with no future time. Don't conditionals have to contain some kind of future event or a tense change?

Explanation

Most 'real' conditionals will have some element of future time. The tense of clauses in conditional sentences is flexible and, as (7), (8) and (9) demonstrate, mixing of the types is common. The examples in (1) show the standard forms often presented in reference books where simple past in the *if*-clause requires *would* or *could* in the main clause and where a past perfect *if*-clause will lead to a perfect tense form in the main.

    If I moved the logo, I would/could create more space. (10)

    If I had moved the logo, I would/could have created more space. (11)

In truth, though, there are no strict tense requirements for forming conditionals and this is evidenced in the three enquiries above. (7) has an *if*-clause in the simple past with a main clause in the perfect tense; (8) has a simple past tense *if*-clause and *will* in the main clause; and (9) has both clauses in the simple past.

(7) relates to an unreal conditional (see **25**) rather than a possible or potential one, because the person is not confrontational and so would not have been able to fulfil the condition. It is reporting an event that has occurred and which is relevant to the discussion, so it contains a perfect form in the main clause.

(8) might be a little difficult to interpret in written form and with no context, but as a spoken response it is unlikely there would be any confusion about the meaning. Someone has made an enquiry on someone else's behalf, and the speaker is pointing out that the registration was quite recent so it might not have been processed yet and therefore the paperwork may not be quite ready.

As pointed out, (9) contains no future time reference. Both clauses are in the past tense. And if a conditional does contain an event relating to the future, then this can appear in either the main clause or the *if*-clause. Here in (12), a future refer-ence occurs in both.

If sleep will help, I'll make sure I get an early night.† (12)

And another thing . . . 24

Some conditionals are more like paired statements with no real conditional element. They might consist of an adage or a saying in the *if*-clause followed by an assertion that is of a comparable nature in the main clause.

If Cheung is a big fish in a small pond, then Sanchez is a whale in a puddle.

25
In an unreal mood

Moods in English indicate the attitude of the writer or speaker through the nature of the verb form that is adopted. Some moods allow a stance or view to be demonstrated. But when the expression is factual, the mood is known as indicative.

She was born in Sweden. (1)

The indicative is by far the most common mood in English. It is used for declarative sentences (statements) and interrogative ones (questions).

—For hypothetical assertions or opinions and conditional situations, the subjunctive mood can be employed. The subjunctive is likely to be found in a subordinate clause rather than in the main clause.

We prefer <u>that she move</u> this meeting to a more suitable time. (2)

—The imperative mood is generally used for commands and direct requests.

Don't change its shape.† (3)

It is also employed in advertising.

Meet Santa   Save the rhino today! (4) (5)

But imperatives can also represent suggestions and polite invitations.

Take a handbook.   Make yourself at home.
Have some time on your own. (6) (7) (8)

◆ ◆ ◆

(9) We insist that he answer this immediately.†

(10) They were governed, as it were, by this informal group.

Student enquiry: I have found two examples where the verb forms do not match the pronouns. In (9), I would expect *answer* to take an *s* because the pronoun is singular (. . . *he answers this immediately*). And in (10), should the writer not be using *was* (*as it was*) to match the singular pronoun instead of plural *were*?

Explanation

These two examples are in the subjunctive mood. When the subjunctive is used, there is no need to inflect the verb in the third person singular; that is why in (9), the noun is written as *answer* and not *answers*. There are a limited number of verbs that the subjunctive can be used with (these include *demand, require, desire* and *prefer*). Sometimes, *should* can be added to the phrase.

> They suggested that he (should) remove his earpiece for the discussion.   (11)

The subjunctive also occurs in certain idiomatic or set expressions (see **Glossary**) where the words that comprise the phrase are fixed and perhaps different from the expected arrangement. In (10), the phrase *as it were* is an idiom in the subjunctive mood (*as it was* would be the expected form, as pointed out above). Phrases like *If I were you* are sometimes labelled the past subjunctive, but this is misleading because they do not relate to past tense. They are unreal conditions that also go by the name of irrealis (see **Glossary**).

Compare the hypothetical example (12) with an example where the subjunctive is unavailable because an action has actually taken place (13).

> If I were strict, then I might have told them to stop.   (12)

> If I was strict, then it was because they needed to be disciplined.   (13)

And another thing . . . 25

One form of the subjunctive creates subject-verb inversion.

> <u>Were</u> I to choose the first option, I might feel a bit better.

A further use is when *be* is employed instead of the usual indicative forms (*am/is/ was/are*). This often occurs in statements of purpose and acknowledgement.

> The message is that they <u>be</u> vigilant at this difficult time.

26
Passives should be actively used

In an active clause, a noun phrase can act as subject and be the thing performing the action. Some active clauses (1i) can be made passive (1ii) by moving the
object to subject position.

The tutors used John's designs.	(1i)
John's designs were used by the tutors.	(1ii)

Often the *by*-phrase (*by the tutors*) at the end can be left out of the sentence. In
(2ii) and (3ii), the subjects of the active constructions (underlined) are omitted
from these passive versions.

We removed the solution from its vessel.	(2i)
The solution was removed from its vessel.	(2ii)
Morgan then moved the decimal point two places to the left.	(3i)
The decimal point was then moved two places to the left.	(3ii)

This is known as an agentless passive. These sentences could contain agents (*by
us / by Morgan*), but there may be a valid reason for not including them. Reasons
include not wishing to identify the agents and the agents not being relevant to
the discussion. But not all clauses have to have an action carried out by a person.
If an action is being performed, then something else can perform it and a person
can receive it.

A pedestrian was hit by a car yesterday in this area.	(4)

In (5), a concept plays this role.

The financiers were largely driven by greed.	(5)

—The passive has an undeserved reputation for supposedly producing weak and
indistinct, even obscure, sentences; this is the reason why developers of gram-
mar-checking software programs place great value on their passive sentence
filters, ones that warn us about the passive voice as if it's a sin and that recom-
mend we adopt an active voice regardless of the context. The truth is the passive

construction has several uses and is effective in certain situations. As mentioned, if the agent is difficult to identify or is irrelevant, then the passive is the logical choice. The form also proves effective when a writer wishes to avoid repetition.

> *We propose a model that can dramatically reduce the waiting time. We take Ranlon and Morgan's (2009) initial structure and add a layer (Figure 3). We designed the model using VectorM.* (6i)

Here, we have three sentences leading with the pronoun *we*. Rephrasing the final sentence (by giving it a passive structure) reduces this repetition and improves the composition.

> *We propose a model that can dramatically reduce the waiting time. We take Ranlon and Morgan's (2009) initial structure and add a layer (Figure 3). The model was designed using VectorM.* (6ii)

—The passive form can actually draw the reader's eye towards key information by emphasising the noun phrase. This proves particularly effective in (7i). The passive form seems to strengthen the pertinent information here (*the thousand villagers*) by fronting it. The active form (7ii) lessens the impact of this key statistic in the sentence.

> *Up to a thousand villagers would be deprived of a vote in this move.* (7i)

> *This move would deprive up to a thousand villagers of the vote.* (7ii)

◆ ◆ ◆

(8) She was pleased to hear that the reviews were positive.

(9) It was assumed by the interviewees that the company was failing.

(10) I can reveal that the money was stolen by the inspector.

Student enquiry: I am trying to put the passive statement in (8) into an active voice but I am not sure how to do this. In (9), although I am having no difficulty changing this sentence into an active one (*The interviewees assumed that the company was failing*), I wondered what action was being expressed . . . is it the fact they are *assuming* something?

I have read that active sentences bring the actor or agent to prominence. But it occurred to me when looking at the passive in (10) that it is emphasising the agent's role better than if it was written in an active way (*The inspector stole the money*).

Explanation

The reason why it is difficult to convert, so to speak, example (8) into an active form is that it is not a passive construction in the first place. It is true that the past tense of *to be* (*was*) appears alongside a past participle (*pleased*), but that does not necessarily indicate that a sentence is passive. The verb is simply joining an adjective complement to its subject. Unfortunately, it is common practice for sentences to be labelled passive simply because they do not look like active ones or they happen to have features of a passive.

Allied to this is the familiar explanation of active and passive being about performing an action and experiencing an action. This, too, is unhelpful and misleading; sometimes there is no action taking place (see also **17**). That is why passive constructions should not be defined in semantic terms. Agents may not be doing anything to anyone in the clause. In (9), it could be argued that no action as such is taking place. It is therefore more helpful to consider passives in a syntactic way, i.e. through analysing their structure and form, not their meaning.

We saw the effectiveness of a noun phrase being fronted for emphasis in (7i). Well, the agent can also be emphasised just as effectively in a passive construction as in an active one. Example (10) is a good example of a fiction writer doing just that, using a passive and emphasising the agent through a delay. This is a natural characteristic of the language, placing the newest information at the end of the sentence, and the passive helps to achieve this.

There are even situations when an active form can appear to take a passive reading. In (11) and (12), the so-called agent cannot perform the action. These sentences have passive appearances, but not the properties of the passive form.

The diagram worked well. (11)

This phone charged quickly. (12)

And another thing . . . 26

Some short passives cannot be changed to active forms.

He was taken hostage in 1997.

27

It doesn't seem active, but it doesn't look passive

Only transitive verbs (verbs said to require a direct object) can occur in a passive clause. And there are some verbs that appear exclusively in the passive.

The CEO was <u>born</u> in the neighbouring town. (1)

While a handful of transitive verbs cannot be made passive.

The scientists <u>lacked</u> evidence for this. (2)

John <u>had</u> two files on the memory stick. (3)

A misconception that occurs with passives is to consider them impersonal or ambiguous versions of the active form. We can illustrate the flaw in this argument using (4) and (5). Now, (4) looks like a passive with no agent and is followed in (5) by what appears to be a more active-sounding alternative, this time with an explicit agent (*we*). But (4) cannot be passive because it contains an intransitive verb (*occur*). Clearly, then, active sentences sometimes sound vague too, having the ability to hide agents or actors. There is in fact no active/passive relationship between these two sentences at all.

<u>A problem occurred</u> over the weekend with the mechanism. (4)

Over the weekend <u>we had a problem</u> with the mechanism. (5)

—A passive clause will always contain a participle. The participle will often appear with a form of the verb *to be*.

The deadline <u>was changed</u> again. (6)

—The verb *to get* also appears in passives in informal writing and speech.

The signs <u>got</u> removed, so they will need replacing. (7)

◆   ◆   ◆

(8) The images need altering.

(9) The teacher had the tutor observed by an inspector.

(10) The goalkeeper was injured.

Student enquiry: I think that examples (8) and (9) are probably passives; yet (8) does not have a past participle, and neither of them contains a form of the verb *to be*, which I thought were the two features of a passive sentence. And in (10) I am not sure whether to label this a passive verb phrase because it seems more like an adjective phrase to me.

Explanation

As mentioned in **26**, it is a common mistake to think that every sentence with a form of the verb *to be* and a participle is passive. It is equally untrue that every passive construction must contain this verb. We have already seen *get* being used in a passive clause (7).

The verb *to need* acts as the finite or tensed main verb in the passive clause in (8). This example also illustrates the fact that not all passive constructions contain a past participle, featuring, as it does, a present one (*altering*).

(9) is actually active in structure but has a passive clause embedded in it (*observed by an inspector*). It, too, contains no form of the verb *to be*. A further example of an embedded passive occurs in (11), where the choice of the active or the passive clause at the end will depend on whether the writer wishes to place emphasis on the fact the IT specialists were the ones changing the design (11i) or on the design being changed (11ii).

> *The manager had the IT specialists change the design.* (11i)
>
> *The manager had the design changed by the IT specialists.* (11ii)

Ambiguity can arise when sentences consist of a linking verb followed by a past participle. This is apparent in (10), where it is unclear whether the phrase is describing an event or action in which the goalkeeper had just been injured in a match (thus making it passive), or a state in which the goalkeeper had an existing injury and was not playing in the match (thus making it active and adjectival).

And another thing . . . 27

Care is required in those instances where the active and the passive counterparts are not equivalent in meaning. In this first set they do have equivalence:

> *Some visitors swapped their vouchers.*
>
> *Vouchers were swapped by some visitors.*

But in this second set there is a subtle difference, or more precisely a different focus, and the outcomes are not identical; they are similar but not identical. The active reveals that not many issues were covered. The passive refers only to the issues not covered and does not speculate on how many issues were covered.

The CEO did not cover many issues.

Many issues were not covered by the CEO.

In this final set, the generalisation in the first example is unavailable in the passive, as not all holes in the ground are created by dogs.

Dogs dig holes in the ground.

*Holes in the ground are dug by dogs.

28
'-ing' terpreting

One of the more complex categorising tasks related to English grammar is labelling words ending with *-ing*. In fact, unless they are common nouns, e.g. *building*, *evening* and *king*, or pure adjectives, e.g. *time-consuming* and *exciting*, the prudent approach is to simply label them *-ing* forms. It would be beneficial, however, to appreciate the differences between so-called gerunds (or verbal nouns) and present participles (or participle adjectives).

—A gerund is said to act like a noun but still retains the essence of the verb from which it derives.

> He enjoys <u>running</u> in the park. (1)

In (1), *running* is classed as a gerund but it has strong verb-like qualities. For one, it is modified by adverbs not adjectives.

> He enjoys running (<u>quickly/fast</u>) in the park. (2)

But if we remove the prepositional phrase *in the park*, the term has a more noun-like quality.

> He enjoys running. (3)

Indeed, a difference in word class may exist in phrases that appear almost indistinguishable. In (4i), *breathing* is functioning as a noun by taking an adjective and in (4ii) as a verb by taking an adverb.

> The third task saw a lot of heavy <u>breathing</u>. (4i)

> The third task saw a lot of <u>breathing</u> heavily. (4ii)

When an *-ing* form has purely noun-like qualities such as that in (4i), it is sometimes known as a deverbal noun (in contrast to a verbal one). This means it has derived from a verb but unlike a gerund shares none of the characteristics of a verb.

Gerunds can occur at the beginning of a sentence and function as the subject. The *-ing* form here in (5) is a gerund because it forms a verb phrase (*watching documentaries*) that then acts like a noun in the sentence. Compare this to the earlier deverbal noun in (4i) which forms a noun phrase (*heavy breathing*), not a verb phrase.

Watching documentaries was another suggestion made by the tutor.   (5)

This *-ing* form (*watching*) can be used to demonstrate the verb/noun dynamic from (6) nominal to (8) verbal, with (7) occupying a middle ground.

I like people watching.   (6)

I like watching.   (7)

I like watching films.   (8)

Present participles also end in *-ing* and appear in the progressive aspect with the verb *to be*.

I am watching films.†   (9)

Participles have adjectival properties. Here, *watching* appears before a noun, modifying it.

The watching children were eager to join in.   (10)

◆ ◆ ◆

(11i) They remembered to mark it.

(11ii) They remembered marking it.

(12i) I continued using the device for ten more minutes.

(12ii) I continued to use the device for ten more minutes.

Student enquiry: I guess it is OK to have two verbs positioned next to each other as in (11) and (12). But I am struggling to understand the difference between the two sets. Is there a choice for some verbs as to whether they are followed by an infinitive or by an *-ing* form?

Explanation

Verbs can come directly after what are known as catenative or chain-forming verbs (see **Glossary**). The second verb will be in the form of an infinitive, a bare infinitive or end in *-ing*. If we look at (11), there is a slight difference in meaning here. (11i) merely implies that they did not forget to mark it, but (11ii) indicates that they recall the actual instance or occasion of marking it. (12i) and (12ii) are examples of the selection being immaterial because both forms have the same meaning.

There are actually five outcomes (13–17) for the form required (of the second verb) after an initial catenative verb. The first verb will govern the usage.

Sometimes an -ing form is needed (13), sometimes an infinitive form is necessary (14), sometimes an infinitive or a bare infinitive (without the to) is available (15), sometimes either an -ing form or an infinitive can be used with no change in meaning (16) and other times either can be employed but with a change in meaning (17).

> We delayed leaving the site as not all the beakers contained specimens.   (13)

> We asked to leave later because of this.   (14)

> They helped (to) move the equipment after the show   (15)

> It began changing/to change.   (16)

> I regret to tell you the project has been cancelled. (I'm sorry to tell you.)   (17i)

> I regret telling you the project has been cancelled. (I wish I hadn't told you.)   (17ii)

The verb to stop allows either an infinitive verb form or an -ing form to appear after it. But like (17), there will be a difference in meaning. The infinitive (18) relates to an action being performed; the -ing form (19), an action that ceases.

> Before you enter the building, stop to take in the views of the gardens.   (18)

> We need to stop worrying about what our colleagues think of our methods.   (19)

And another thing . . . 28

Adjectives can usually take infinitive forms as complements. An exception is worth. Understandably, then, a common mistake is using the infinitive form.

> *This is worth to consider as a subtopic.

> This is worth considering as a subtopic.

Worth requires an -ing form and behaves a lot like a preposition. Here, it serves as complement to a noun phrase.

> It is certainly worth a look.

29

Masquerading as modals

Auxiliary verbs and modal verbs help to express tense and mood. They often support the main verb in a sentence. In (1), the modal verb *can* is assisting the main verb *try*; and in (2), the auxiliary *have* is in the supporting role.

I can try again in the morning.† (1)

I have tried on several occasions without success. (2)

Modals and auxiliaries commonly appear in questions.

Would you leave the company if this policy was pursued? † (3)

Can they replace the signs as well? (4)

—A key syntactic point relating to modals is that the main verb that follows them does not change form. Ordinarily, in the third person singular, an *s* would be added (5ii). But the verb remains in its base form after a modal (5iii).

First person   *I clean the exterior as well.* (5i)

Third person   *He cleans the exterior as well.* (5ii)

Third person with modal   *He can clean the exterior as well.* (5iii)

—In semantic terms, modal verbs often state the likelihood of something happening (6) or the ability or requirement of something (7). This possibility and necessity is often referred to as modality.

We might do a further test on Tuesday. (6)

I will deliver this tomorrow. (7)

One type of modality relates to whether the proposition could be considered true or false.

He might need some training. (8)

They may need an extra day to finish this. (9)

Another type relates to an action being performed at some point in the future.

You must change the content of that section.† (10)

You may enter the room now.† (11)

—Sometimes, the meaning of a modal relates neither to a true/false proposition nor the performing of a future action.

Malcolm can code using the old and the new language. (12)

The type of modality in (12) relates more to a characteristic ability or a property of the subject.

◆ ◆ ◆

(13) I had a strange experience at that company.†

(14) They need not hold the same nationality.

(15) I daren't imagine how many people were affected.†

(16) And he dares to do this in a meeting!†

(17) I might as well.†

Student enquiry: I notice that (13) contains an auxiliary verb (*had*). But where is the main verb in this sentence? In (14), the main verb is clearly *hold* but there is another verb (*need*) in the sentence. I didn't think that *need* could be used as an auxiliary verb though it seems to be acting like one here. And in (15), I know that *daren't* stands for *dare not* but can dare be an auxiliary/modal too?

I am not sure how to categorise the same verb in (16), because it is coming before an infinitive (which a modal cannot do), so is it an auxiliary or the main verb? And like (13), (17) does not seem to have a main verb, only a modal.

Explanation

The auxiliary verbs (*be, do, have*) are able to perform the role of main verb in a sentence. In (13), the past form of *have* is not acting as an auxiliary but as a main verb. In fact, a verb can appear as the main verb and as an auxiliary verb in the same sentence.

He was being kind for a change.† (18)

I have had my feedback already.† (19)

In (14) and (15), the verbs *need* and *dare* are acting as modals. Although not commonly thought of as modals, they can perform this role but only in negative (non-affirmative) sentences. If the statement is an affirmative one, then these verbs will be functioning as the main verb. In (20), *need* is the main verb, and in (21) *need* is a modal, as it is in (14).

They need evidence of this. (20)

They need not worry about that yet. (21)

In fact, *need* can occur alongside *will* or *may* to create a rare double modal.

They may need never work again. (22)

In (16), *dare* comes before an infinitive phrase because it is acting as the main verb in the sentence. (17) is a response to a statement that would have contained a main verb. The response omits the verb because it is implied. For instance, the initial remark could have been either

I might change before I go out.†

or   *Are you going to tell them?* †

The response of (17) with the ellipsis is now interpretable despite having no main verb.

I might as well.†

And another thing . . . 29

Ought is another verb that has a slight claim to being considered a modal. But it differs from the others in that it has to be followed by *to*, leading some to speculate whether it is a main verb taking an infinitive as a complement rather than a true modal.

But like a modal it does not change its form and it cannot be used with any other modal. *Ought to* is similar in meaning to *should*, and in fact *should* can act as its replacement in a negative tag question.

There <u>ought to</u> be someone facilitating this, <u>shouldn't</u> there? †

Let is a further example of a verb with the potential to perform as a modal (when it is a contraction and used for making offers, suggestions and to oblige), as it relies upon the presence of a main verb.

Let's <u>change</u> the title.†

Let's not <u>tell</u> them yet.†

30
The possibilities of *may*

Typical applications of the modal verb *may* include showing possibility (1) and giving permission for an action (2).

He may cope with this; we will have to wait and see. (1)

You may enter.† (2)

Technically these both relate to possibility, but the latter is more a confirmation or approval that something can take place (*must* is used for necessary actions). In (2) *may* is equivalent to *can*, as it is when someone issues a refusal (3).

You may not talk during this event.† (3i)

You cannot talk during this event.† (3ii)

(See **39** for its role in negation.)

There is also equivalence between these two modals when the purpose of something is being shown or expressed.

This is carried out so staff may/can continue working on the site. (4)

But when the truth of the proposition is not clear, as is the case in (1) (*He may cope with this . . .*), *can* is not then an equivalent term.

—A further use of *may* is to add a level of politeness to questions or statements.

May I use this textbook for a bit? † (5)

If I may, there seems to be some confusion as to the goals of the project.† (6)

◆ ◆ ◆

(7) Certain ticket holders may view the performance from the platform.

(8) You may be a child, but that does not excuse this behaviour.†

Student enquiry: I am interested in the level of certainty in (7). Does *may* have the equivalence of *can*? Or is it just a possibility with no certainty, like in *They may go to the concert tomorrow*? And in (8), I'm not sure I understand the phrase *you may be a child*. Surely it is beyond doubt that the person being discussed is a child, so why use *may*?

Explanation

(7) demonstrates quite a formal use of *may* to indicate permission. It does have the equivalence of *can* in this instance (as it does in (2)). It is used in this way when the proposition is almost certainly true.

> *The director may be found in the school office on your left.*†   (9)

If we modify this example, we can create a sentence that instead indicates possibility and with the equivalence not of *can* but *might*.

> *The director may be in his office.*†   (10)

The distinction between the two modals is further illustrated here. (11) indicates that the director could be available but, equally, could be busy. This is the same level of possibility as found in (1) and in (10), where the truth is unknown. But (12) indicates that the director is available if required (and so the truth is known here), and this is a statement likely to be uttered by a secretary or someone who is aware of the director's schedule and availability.

> *The director may be available.*   (11)

> *The director can be available.*   (12)

Similarly, *may* is preferred to *can* for guidelines and when stating rules and regulations. It is also used in a subordinate clause to acknowledge that something is true (often like a concession) before going on to make a point regardless of that fact. This accounts for its seemingly exceptional use in (8).

And another thing . . . 30

Unlike many modals (except perhaps *ought*), the negative form of *may* is rarely contracted.

> *You can try but you mayn't have long.*†

31
Shall I or will I?

According to standard reference books, the modal *shall* is employed with first person pronouns when discussing the future (1, 2). For second and third person pronouns, this changes to *will* (3, 4).

I shall be leaving for the conference at 2 p.m. (1)

We shall try to get our draft submitted by tomorrow. (2)

You will be meeting them at the airport.† (3)

They will be disappointed when you tell them. (4)

The opposite is said to be true for obligation or expressing that something should happen.

I will guarantee that these folders remain closed. (5)

We will look after these artefacts for the time being. (6)

You shall not begin until the buzzer sounds.† (7)

They shall only receive numerical data for this task. (8)

AmE is much more relaxed on this issue, and even British writers no longer follow these rules dogmatically.

—But a comparison can be drawn for the modals *shall* and *should*, the latter having less force and obligation than the former. To illustrate, in (9) the speaker is making a suggestion; in (10), this becomes an instruction with the change of modal.

It's getting late. We should finish this in the morning.† (9)

It's getting late. We shall finish this in the morning.† (10)

This next comparison of the two modals relates to certainty of an event. In (11), the speaker is only hopeful of arriving on time and chooses *should*. In (12), the speaker is more confident of their punctuality and selects *shall*.

We should arrive at the conference by 2. (11)

We shall arrive at the conference by 2. (12)

◆ ◆ ◆

(13) The committee shall withhold this amount until evidence is provided.

(14) Shall I move them to our headquarters? †

Student enquiry: I have always assumed that *will* was equivalent to *shall* and the two could substitute for each other. I can see this is true in (13) although I am not sure of the reason behind the choice of *shall* here. But in (14), the use of *will* instead of *shall* would surely change the meaning of the question!

Explanation

It is fine to replace *shall* with *will* in (13). The reason *shall* has been chosen is that it is used in legal and official documents such as contracts to provide a more authoritative tone. (14) is a good example of *will* and *shall* not being interchangeable. When asking a question in the first person, as occurs in (14), *shall* is required, not *will*. Conversely, when something is asked of someone in the mode of an instruction or order, *will* is appropriate but not *shall*.

Will you keep up with the others.†	**Shall you keep . . .*	(15)
Will you close the door behind you.†	**Shall you close . . .*	(16)

And another thing . . . 31

The modal can often be repeated when responding to a question. But this is less true of *shall*, especially when the aim of the enquiry is to seek guidance.

Will I be able to check my emails on site?	*Yes, you will.†*
Shall I put them on our intranet?	**Yes, you shall †*

32

Does *do* double up?

As shown in **29**, the verb *to do* can perform the role of main verb in a sentence (1). It also functions as an auxiliary verb (2).

She <u>does</u> the dancing and I <u>do</u> the choreography. (1)

They <u>do</u> leave things to the last minute, unfortunately. (2)

Naturally, when it is the main verb it follows auxiliaries and modals.

They <u>can do</u> this better with some further training. (3)

And as an auxiliary it can add emphasis.

I <u>did</u> change the design on the new model. (4)

—*Do* often occurs in imperative sentences (orders and commands), both positive (5) and negative (6).

Do keep me in mind. (5)

Don't use those machines.† (6)

—*Do* can also be employed as a substitute (7ii) for an earlier verb or verb phrase to avoid repetition, like that occurring in (7i). This is perhaps more common in BrE than in AmE, where the second instance of the verb is likely to be omitted.

Bill spoke for longer than he had <u>spoken</u> the time before. (7i)

Bill spoke for longer than he had <u>done</u> the time before. (7ii)

◆ ◆ ◆

(8) I know they do not do this.

(9) Do you do different varieties, or is it just this flavour?†

Student enquiry: In (8), there are two instances of the verb *to do*; one is positive and the other is negative. I wondered whether they would just cancel each other out here. The first instance, the auxiliary I am guessing, does not seem to have any real meaning attached to it. Equally, is it normal to use two instances of the verb in the way (9) has done?

Explanation

In both (8) and (9) *do* is performing a necessary role.

In the absence of any other modal, it supports the negating word *not* in (8). But when *not* precedes infinitive forms and participles, it will not require the support of *do*. Compare (8) with (10).

> *I know not to do this.*   (10)

In (9), the initial instance of the verb is performing a role to satisfy the grammatical requirements of the sentence. Because it is difficult to pin down the exact meaning of *do* here, it is referred to as dummy *do* or a dummy operator (see also **48**). The second verb does not have to be *do* in this example. *Have* is also an option.

> *Do you have different varieties . . .*   (11)

It is even possible for the verb to appear successively.

> *Oh yes, do do this if you are able to.†*   (12)

And another thing . . . 32

The verb can also be employed alongside *be* in imperatives that can sound rather frank or terse.

> *Do be professional when you speak to them.†*

> *Don't be using those images in the real presentation.†*

Understanding 16–32

Note: some questions may have more than one correct answer. Some questions may have no correct or no incorrect answers.

16. A. Which of these terms represents a homonym?

fair   produce   drive

B. Which of these statements about identical noun and verb forms is true?

They are always pronounced the same.

The initial syllable is stressed for the noun.

The initial syllable is stressed for the verb.

17. A. Which of these is an intransitive verb?

love   respond   edit

B. When might a transitive verb NOT take a direct object?

when the identity of the object is clear from the context

when the verb appears in a conditional

when the verb expresses an action

18. A. Which of these verb forms is not a past participle?

wrote   risen   left

B. Which of these statements is true of an irregular verb?

The past participle will not end in –ed.

The past tense and past participle will have different forms.

The present participle will end in –ing.

19. A. Which of these spellings would you NOT expect to find in a British textbook?

canceled   developing   worshipping

B. What is the correct spelling for a term describing goods or people illegally moved around?

traffiked   trafflced   trafficked   traficked

20. A. Which of these phrases shows an example of the historic present?

then I walk in   then I stopped quickly   then I'll move it back

B. *Harry was working there when we left.* Which of the following statements may be true?

Harry works at the company.   Harry left the company after them.

Harry used to work at the company.

21. A. Which of these sentences could be changed to the present tense?

Sari used these effects.   I will move it later.   John edited it last time.

B. Which of these sentences is employing the habitual present?

Bonnie drives us to the meetings.   I can drive us to the meeting.

Bonnie drives us on Monday.

22. A. Which of these verb phrases is in the past perfect progressive?

They had been checking this.   He will have checked this.

I have been reading.

B. *A continuous action that was completed before another past action began* refers to which tense?

past perfect progressive   past perfect   past progressive

23. A. When might backshifting not be applied?

when the utterance is present tense

when the utterance is still valid or relevant

when the writer doubts the truth of the utterance

B. Which verb cannot be inverted (i.e. come before the subject) when reporting direct speech?

admit   say   tell   reveal

24. A. Which of these sentences is considered a zero conditional?

When I was hungry, I should have eaten.

When I am hungry, I eat.

If I eat, I won't be hungry.

B. When the *if*-clause of a conditional contains a future time reference . . .

the main clause will not contain a future time reference.

the main clause may or may not contain a future time reference.

the *if-* clause cannot contain a reference to future time.

25. A. Which of these phrases is in the subjunctive mood?

If he were here   To be or not to be   Beware of the dog.

B. Which of these statements is incorrect?

The imperative mood can be used for suggestions.

The so-called 'past subjunctive' does not relate to the past tense.

The imperative mood is used for questions.

26. A. Which of these phrases is a passive construction?

The design changed several times.   The student got removed eventually.

The teacher refused to agree to this.

B. And which of these phrases is passive?

The manager got his revenge on them.

The manager was annoyed to hear this.

The manager moved the meeting to later.

27. A. Which of these verbs never occurs in a passive construction?

born   lack   need

B. Which of the following are true?

A passive clause must contain a participle.

A passive clause must contain a form of the verb to be.

A passive clause cannot always be made active.

28. A. Which of these verbs can be followed by a bare infinitive?

ask   delay   help

B. Which of the following sentences are written correctly?

They helped fix the machine.   They helped fixing the machine.

They helped to fix the machine.

29. A. In which sentence does *have* perform the role of the main verb?

I have not replaced it.   I have tried this.   I had an opportunity to go.

B. In which of the following is *need* being used as a modal?

Their need is greater than ours.   They need to alter their approach.

They need not alter their approach.

30. A. In which sentence is *may* not necessarily equivalent to *can*?

She may be available.   You may not leave yet.

They may wait in the office.

B. In which situations is *may* equivalent to *can*?

when indicating permission   when issuing a refusal

when showing possibility

31. A. When might *shall* be preferred to *will*?

to express hope   to ask a question in the first person

to ask a question in the third person

B. Which modal tends to have the least force or obligation?

should   shall   will

32. A. In which of these sentences is *do* being used as a dummy?

You could do this.   Do you have others?   I do try.

B. When might *do* be required to support *not* in a sentence?

when *not* precedes a participle   when *not* precedes an infinitive form

when *not* precedes a linking verb

C. PREPOSITIONS, ADJECTIVES, AND ADVERBS

33
Ending the preposition debate

The selection of a preposition may be governed by the term preceding it when the preposition's role is functional. For instance, *similar, likelihood* and *accompanied* happen to take specific prepositions.

This is similar to the scheme in 1999. (1)

The likelihood of this happening is remote. (2)

They were accompanied by their respective teachers. (3)

When the preposition is used lexically or factually, the meaning (which will relate to one-, two-, or three-dimensional space) determines the choice.

We waited behind the main building for them to arrive. (4)

These islands are all below sea level. (5)

There may be a more figurative (i.e. not literal) reference to location or place.

They are moving towards a crossroads in the negotiations. (6)

We are behind our manager 100%.† (7)

I am not into these topics really. (8)

The gerund will influence the selection of the preposition in these opening clauses, the meaning equivalent to *as a result of.*

On reading the report, the director chose to reinstate the employee. (9)

In moving this, they have managed to create valuable space. (10)

—Some words have a relationship with more than one preposition, in which case context will likely determine the selection. In (11), selecting *for* or *of* will depend on whether the speaker is focusing on the well-being of the person (i) or the thoughtful action (ii).

It was good for them to organise the trip. (11i)

It was good of them to organise the trip. (11ii)

—Although prepositions are a main word class in English, there is no such class as postpositions in the language. The only candidates would be terms like *ago*, and *notwithstanding* following a noun phrase, but these are generally considered to be an adverb and an adjective respectively.

It occurred around <u>two weeks ago</u>. (12)

These objectives <u>notwithstanding</u>, the proposal will require significant amendments. (13)

Prepositions that occur at the end of a sentence are not classed as postpositions either (but they are said to be postposed). Their position (i.e. the reason for the *pre-* part of their name) relates to the complement to which they are attached and not whether they appear near the beginning or near the end of the sentence. When phrases are fronted, i.e. moved to the 'front' of the sentence, this can leave the preposition stranded at the end (14ii).

I can think <u>of</u> two instances. (14i)

There are two instances I can think <u>of</u>. (14ii)

Equally, prepositions can be fronted as seen in (15i). Sometimes, this produces a more eloquent style.

<u>At</u> which institution did he study? † (15i)

Compare: *Which institution did he study <u>at</u>?* † (15ii)

But it would be wrong to think that all sentences can or should be structured this way. For one thing, this fronting is not always viable.

What did he say that <u>for</u>? †   **<u>For</u> what did he say that?* (16)

Other times the fronting just sounds awkward or overly affected (17ii).

What are you using that <u>with</u>? † (17i)

Compare: *<u>With</u> what are you using that?* † (17ii)

—The prepositions in so-called prepositional verbs (18ii) are sometimes labelled 'postpositions', but their nature is largely idiomatic (see **Glossary**) and linked only to the verbs they are in partnership with. It seems to make little sense to create a new word class or to think of them as anything other than prepositions (see **And another thing**).

You can work <u>at the desk</u>.† (18i)

You should <u>look at</u> the weather now! † (18ii)

◆ ◆ ◆

(19) Can you see what the lever is for?†

(20) No, it is not really heard of.†

Student enquiry: I was always told that you cannot end a sentence with a preposition, but both (19) and (20) finish with them. Are there occasions when this rule does not need to be followed, then?

Explanation

An obvious talking point regarding prepositions is the so-called 'rule' that you cannot finish a sentence with one. This guideline was created and gained in popularity from a misguided attempt to force the grammar rules of Latin onto English and the publication of some dubious prescriptive grammar guides in the early twentieth century. It has already been shown that there are several situations where a preposition cannot be fronted and where, if a phrase is fronted, it may finish up at the end of the sentence.

Indeed, there is a reason why a famous Irish pop group chose not to adopt 'I still haven't found for what I am looking' as the title of their song.

In practice, there is nothing wrong with ending a sentence with one. In fact, it is quite natural to do so in relative clauses and in questions (19). Certainly, prepositions that have a tendency to form partnerships (or collocate) with other terms (commonly *on*, *in*, *at*, *of*) will often be stranded at the end of the sentence, with no available means of fronting (20).

And another thing . . . 33

Some phrases that comprise a verb + preposition can be split up by an object.

They should also take off their jewellery.

They should also take their jewellery off.

These are often called phrasal verbs, and the prepositional word is considered an adverb in this construction. It is also commonly referred to as a particle (see **Glossary**). But some verb + preposition forms cannot be split up like this. For the purpose of comparison,

A *take off* = verb + adverb (particle)   *take (something) off*

B *depend on* = verb + preposition   **depend (something) on*

Arguments have been made for particles to be seen as either a subclass of adverbs or a subclass of prepositions (the latter camp would therefore recognise both types [A and B] as containing prepositions). This latter view is certainly a simpler categorisation, because these words are already familiar as prepositions. They are also acting as a complement to the verb, which adverbs tend not to do (adverbs are usually adjuncts [see **Glossary**]). It may be easier to think of these particles as a subclass of prepositions that do not take complements and perform like adverbs than as a very limited member of the adverb class. Many adverbs can modify verbs, adjectives, other adverbs and even whole sentences. But *on, up* and *with* have none of this versatility, as the following rather puerile syntactic test demonstrates:

Modifying adjectives: *They were <u>exactly</u> right.*   **They were <u>on/up/with</u> right.*

Modifying verbs: *She <u>steadily</u> improved it.*   **She <u>on/up/with</u> improved it.*

Modifying other adverbs: *It works <u>quite</u> poorly.*   **It works <u>on/up/with</u> poorly.*

34
Attributing a position to an adjective

When adjectives appear directly before the noun that they are modifying or clarifying, they are said to be in an attributive position (1i) (see **Glossary**). Adjectives
can also be used predicatively, that is, after a linking or copular verb (1ii). Observe
the position of *finished* here.

> The <u>finished product</u> was delivered to the company with a week to spare.   (1i)

> This one <u>is finished</u> but those are incomplete.†   (1ii)

Ordinarily, a modifying word that comes after the verb would be an adverb (e.g.
He walks calmly). But, and as seen in (1ii), copular verbs such as *be, appear, look,
seem*, can be followed by adjectives (e.g. *He appears calm*).

—Some adjectives have restrictions on where they can be placed in a clause. The
adjectives *sheer* and *sole* can only be used attributively.

> The <u>sheer magnitude</u> of the industry is a daunting prospect for these
> new entrants.   (2)

> Contact was made with the <u>sole tenant</u> of the property.   (3)

Others are restricted to the predicative position.

> The pupils are <u>afraid</u> of the new tutor.   (4)

The afraid pupils

Some present participles (5) and past participles (6) can be used attributively.

> The <u>moving vehicle</u> was then recorded for 30 seconds.   (5)

> To achieve the <u>required score</u>, there will need to be evidence of critical
> engagement.   (6)

—Adjectives that have a temporary or momentary sense attached to them tend
not to be used attributively. That is why feelings and emotions are unlikely to
premodify.

The participants <u>are now eating</u> in the common room.† (7)

The eating participants . . .

But an adjective describing a more permanent or fixed state can be used in either position.

This report <u>is extensive</u> and covers all the key issues. (8i)

This <u>extensive report</u> covers all the key issues. (8ii)

◆ ◆ ◆

(9) It did not take them long to contact the managers concerned / the concerned managers.

(10) We spoke to the injured people / the people injured.

(11) We will then hear an address from the governor general.

Student enquiry: In these examples an adjective is being used directly after a noun. I thought that an adjective had to be used either directly before the noun (*excited people*) or directly after a linking verb (*the people are excited*). Also, is there any difference in meaning between the two options in (9) and (10)?

Another instance of an adjective being used directly after a noun is in (11), where the noun *governor* is premodifying the adjective *general*.

Explanation

Adjectives can occupy a postpositive position, which means they appear directly after the noun. In (9), the position of the adjective does affect the meaning of the sentence. The *managers concerned* refers to the relevant managers or the managers that are involved. But as a premodifier, *concerned* has the meaning of worried or troubled, so *concerned managers* will be worried or troubled ones.

In (10), the adjective can be used before or after the noun with no change in meaning. Both *injured people* and *people injured* are semantically equivalent. There are instances, then, where an adjective can have a single interpretation (like with *injured* but not *concerned*); often though, when the adjective comes before the noun (13), it will relate to a condition that is more permanent in nature than if it came after.

Obviously, *people sensitive* should make other arrangements. (12)

Obviously, *sensitive people* should make other arrangements. (13)

(12) refers to people who are experiencing a temporary state of sensitivity based on the current situation or event. So, this is a warning for those that are sensitive

to the specific thing being discussed and for them to make other arrangements. (13), on the other hand, refers to people who are generally sensitive—people who have sensitivity to things as a characteristic.

(11) features a set phrase in which an adjective occurs directly after a noun. Set phrases of this nature are often loan words (from French) or archaic forms. Principally, they are positions of rank or legal terms.

> *lieutenant general   force majeure   court-martial   femme fatale*

Another adjective that can appear after the noun is *aplenty*. In fact, it is limited to this position.

> *There was talent aplenty at the previous conference.* (14)

There are even occasions when the adjective follows the noun but the modifying roles are reversed. Here in (15), it is the noun that is modifying the head adjective.

> *It was not just loud; it was rock concert loud.*† (15)

And another thing . . . 34

An interesting and sometimes creative use of the language is the phrasal compound adjective. In the second example, a comparative phrase has been moved to the front of the noun phrase.

> *The length was far longer than originally planned.*

> *It was a far longer length than originally planned.*

This fronting is not possible when the phrase contains a complement.

> *The student is best at solo projects.*

> **A best at solo projects student.*

Premodification of the noun can take extreme forms in informal texts and in fiction writing, with often a frenzy of hyphens applied.

> *It was another one of his ten-miles-but-feels-like-seventy road trips.*

35

Getting adjectives in order

When multiple modifiers are linked to a noun there is a general hierarchy. Quantity tends to precede quality, which precedes size.

> <u>Three new large</u> cabinets are required for the library. (1)

Comparatives and superlatives precede modifiers that have non-gradable properties (see **36** and **Glossary**) such as materials and adjectives derived from proper nouns. Here in (2), the superlative comes before the nationality.

> The <u>quickest Chinese</u> athlete clocked a time of 10.29 seconds. (2)

Adjectives denoting nations and nationalities may be further qualified; here, there is pre- and post-modification of British.

> We visited a <u>small British manufacturing</u> company for the final case study. (3)

—When a noun is being modified by a colour and a property of that colour, then the property will come first and the colour will be closest to the noun.

> <u>Saturated yellow</u> rectangles featured heavily in his work. (4)

> It contains a set of <u>translucent blue</u> beads. (5)

◆ ◆ ◆

(6) Vintage American cars are particularly common in the capital of the country.

(7) American vintage cars are unlikely to be as reliable.

Student enquiry: I am not sure what determines the positions of the modifiers *vintage* and *American* in (6) and (7). Can they really be used in either order, and if so, is there then a difference in meaning between them?

Explanation

Certain modifiers can show flexibility in their position in relation to other modifiers, but much will depend on the required emphasis. For the examples shown, if the point relates to vintage cars as opposed to newer cars, then (6) is the better option. But if the emphasis is on the contrast between American cars that are vintage and, say, British cars that are vintage, then (7) is more appropriate. This choice is perhaps more apparent in the following example, where *haunted* is gradable and the focal point in (8) but non-gradable and not the focus in (9). The emphasis, then, tends to fall on the initial modifiers.

> *Maldron Manor is considered a (very) <u>haunted</u> Scottish house.* (8)

> *We have compiled a list of <u>Scottish</u> haunted houses.* (9)

It is possible to modify the initial adjective in (9) with *very* but this would be considered informal usage and perhaps jocular in nature (*Oh, it was a very Scottish haunted house* †).

And another thing . . . 35

Commas are only required between adjectives of the same type. In this first example, *lively* and *animated* are considered to be in the same category (qualities of the discussion) and so are separated by a comma. The modifiers *post-meeting* (timing of the discussion) and *student* (type of discussion) follow, without the need for punctuation.

> *It was a <u>lively, animated</u> post-meeting student discussion.*

And sometimes punctuation is necessary for avoiding ambiguity. As this next example demonstrates, with no hyphen it may be difficult to surmise whether we have a compound that is modifying the head noun (*cross-country* modifying *runner*) or a single word adjective modifying a compound containing two nouns (*cross* modifying *country runner*).

> *I met a cross country runner there.*

Is this, then, someone who runs cross-country or a country runner who is annoyed? A hyphen can be added to achieve the first meaning (*cross-country runner*) while a comma would be needed for the second (*cross, country runner*).

36

Quite ungradable adjectives

Comparative adjectives end in -er and compare one noun with another noun, that is, two items of comparison.

Sally is quicker at this than Suzy is. (1)

Technically, superlatives should compare at least three nouns.

Out of all of them, Hana is the quickest. (2)

There are some adjectives that do not inflect in the way that *quick* does and instead require the adverbs *more/less* (for the comparative) and *most/least* (for the superlative).

The second lecture was more interesting than the first one. (3)

The Japanese exhibition is the most interesting one here. (4)

—There is a mistaken belief that -er is added to all one-syllable adjectives to form the comparative. But this inflection (-er) may not be available for absolute adjectives of one syllable that take comparatives in informal usage (such as *lost*), or when the adjective derives from a past participle (*curved*).

*I think by the end he was loster than I was. (more lost)

*This new design was curveder than the original. (more curved)

Some adjectives neither follow an inflection pattern nor take *more/most*.

That is a good option. / That is a better option. / That is the best option.

—Not all adjectives are gradable. Some cannot be measured for their degree or intensity and are therefore non-gradable. This is true of adjectives that are extremes, adjectives that classify something and absolute adjectives (those considered to be definite or absolute states). Consequently, non-gradable adjectives do not have comparative and superlative forms. This also means they cannot be modified by grading adverbs such as *very, slightly* and *extremely*.

The food was excellent.   (5i)

*The food was very excellent.   (5ii)

This suggested scheme is impossible.   (6i)

*This suggested scheme is more impossible than the other one.   (6ii)

◆   ◆   ◆

(7) The second outcome is likelier / more likely.

(8) This is pretty impossible, if I am honest.†

Student enquiry: The adjective *likely* has two available comparative options in (7). Is it possible for an adjective to take either, does it depend on context or is one correct and the other incorrect? In (8), the non-gradable absolute adjective *impossible* is being modified by an adverb. Is this informal or colloquial usage?

Explanation

Likely belongs to a group of adjectives that can take either an inflection or the adverbs *more/most* for forming their comparative and superlative. The writer/ speaker can therefore select either in (7). Note also that *likely* can be both an adjective (meaning *probable*) and an adverb (meaning *probably*). Other adjectives that provide a choice include *quiet, simple* and *clever*.

He is the most clever / cleverest engineer I have encountered.   (9)

There is no difference in meaning between the options.

(8) is indeed an informal and likely spoken instance of a non-gradable adjective being modified. This would not be suitable for formal writing but is common in dialogue. The adverbs *fairly, pretty, slightly* and *quite* are often found modifying both types of adjective (gradable and non-gradable) and, though not intensifiers, can give extra impact (in a subtle way) to a statement. The following examples (10–12) demonstrate that grading adverbs are now frequently used with non-gradable adjectives in spoken English.

Yeah, it was <u>quite enormous</u> when we opened it up.†   (10)

I think it was <u>rather perfect</u> actually.†   (11)

What they asked us to do was <u>slightly ridiculous</u>.†   (12)

And another thing . . . 36

A few terms that appear to be comparative forms (ending as they do in -*er*) are not in fact related to their stems in this way.

Inner is not the comparative form of *in*.

Outer is not the comparative form of *out*.

Upper is not the comparative form of *up*.

But, *lower* is the comparative form of *low*.

37
Adverbs disguised as adjectives

Many, but certainly not all, adverbs end in *-ly*. These adverbs can reveal how something was done or the way it was done.

> He is a *careful* person and he attached it *carefully*. (1)

> The delivery time is *quick* and my previous package did come *quickly*. (2)

But this description does not stand for all cases. If adjective and adverb forms do exist, then they may not be of the *careful/carefully* type where the adverb is expressing that something is being done in the mode of the adjective. Indeed, there are instances where an adverb may have little or no relation to its stem.

> The temperature is quite *high*. (3i)

> This is *highly* irregular. (3ii)

> The resource is *scarce* in the north of the island. (4i)

> I was *scarcely* able to grip the rope it was so cold. (4ii)

Others are identical in form. Here, (5i) is the adjective and (5ii) is the adverb. *Hardly* is an unrelated adverb.

> It was a *hard* decision to make. (5i)

> I had to admit that he worked *hard* in the end. (5ii)

Late and *early* are further examples where the adjective (6i, 7i) and adverb (6ii, 7ii) have the same spelling. Again, *lately* is an unrelated adverb.

> I think this one was a *late* arrival.† (6i)

> No, this student arrived *late*.† (6ii)

> It will be an *early* start next week.† (7i)

> I am hoping to leave *early* today.† (7ii)

◆ ◆ ◆

(8) They delivered this to me daily.

(9) The daily newsletter ceased when the department was taken over.

(10) There was a strangely quiet atmosphere in the building.

(11) I think this was carried out wrong.

Student enquiry: I know that *daily* is an adverb in (8), but what is it modifying in this sentence? In (9), the same adverb seems to be modifying a noun. In (10), the adverb *strangely* is modifying yet another word class, this time an adjective. So, can adverbs modify any type of word?

If *wrongly* is the adverb form of the adjective *wrong*, why is the adjective used in (11) when it is clearly modifying a verb phrase *carried out*? Do you do something *wrongly* or do something *wrong*, or are both OK?

Explanation

In (8), the adverb *daily* is modifying the past tense verb form *delivered*. In (9), *daily* is not an adverb but an adjective that is modifying the noun *newsletter*. As was the case in (6) and (7), the adjective and adverb forms are the same.

Adverbs can modify adjectives and even other adverbs (see **33**). The adverb in (10) is modifying the adjective *quiet*.

In (11), *wrong* is actually an adverb. Interestingly, *wrong* can be an adverb (11), an adjective (12), or a noun (13).

> That was a wrong move. (12)

> She saw wrong in everything he did. (13)

In fact, this is a term with two adverb forms (*wrong* and *wrongly*). The only restriction of use is that whereas *wrong* can only come after the verb, *wrongly* can occur before or after it.

> *This has been wrong marked. (14i)

> This has been wrongly marked. (14ii)

It is also worth pointing out that adverbs with two forms (such as *quick/quickly*, *cheap/cheaply* and *slow/slowly*) will have different comparative forms (15ii and 16ii).

> Group B completed it quick. (15i)

> Group B completed it quicker (than Group A). (15ii)

> Group B completed it quickly. (16i)

> Group B completed it more quickly (than Group A). (16ii)

And another thing . . . 37

Although the student was misled in (9) into thinking that an adverb was modifying a noun (when, in fact, it was an adjective), it is possible for adverbs and adverbial phrases to modify nouns. The modification will always take place after the noun.

Teachers <u>nationally</u> are asking these same questions.

Her absence <u>yet</u> again indicates this.

In these next examples of adverbs modifying nouns, their character has much in common with the equivalent prepositional forms, and an argument could perhaps be made for labelling them as such (see also **33**).

The weather <u>outside</u> is frightful.†

The view <u>above</u> is slightly obscured.

38

Time adverbs that appear everywhere

Adverbs of time are a rather diverse group. Some do have the common *-ly* ending (e.g. *initially, recently*), but others may only be recognised as belonging to the class from their function or their position in the sentence.

He might visit there <u>again</u>. (1)

We'll speak <u>soon</u>.† (2)

I am moving <u>tomorrow</u>.† (3)

(3) is a good example of word category or class being determined by function. In some instances, *tomorrow* is considered a noun (4), as it refers to an exclusive time. But in (3) it is labelled an adverb because it is modifying the verb. There are two competing arguments here. One is to take word meaning into account when classifying and, in this specific case, to consider *tomorrow* a noun or noun phrase regardless of its role in a sentence. The other is to look at individual contexts and to label according to the way the word is performing in the sentence.

<u>Tomorrow</u> is the deadline. (4)

The examples above (1–3) indicate that time adverbs often occur at the end of the sentence. But they can appear (usually alongside a comma) at the beginning for emphasis (see also **40**).

<u>Later</u>, I returned to the site to collect the remaining data. (5)

<u>Initially</u>, there was no cause for concern. (6)

◆ ◆ ◆

(7) I later stopped to consider the meaning of this.

(8) They have not yet responded to this comment.

(9) She may yet decide to go.

Student enquiry: Given what I have read about where time-related adverbs appear in a sentence, I am surprised by the position of *later* in (7). It occurs before the verb instead of after or at the start of the sentence. And in (8) and (9), the adverb *yet* appears in the middle of these examples, after a negative and a modal respectively, and not at the end or at the beginning.

Explanation

Adverbs ending in *-ly* tend to be more flexible than adverbs without this suffix in where they can appear in a sentence. A notable exception to this is the time adverb *later*, which can go at the beginning (5), at the end, or before the main verb in a sentence (7). When occurring before the main verb, it makes the sentence more formal and is often used for reporting a sequence of events.

When relating to time, *yet* represents another versatile adverb able to occupy several positions. It frequently occurs in negative sentences (8) and after modals when discussing future possibility (9). And it is considered a coordinator rather than an adverb when occurring at the beginning of a dependent clause (10).

I found it difficult, yet I persevered.   (10)

And another thing . . . 38

The adverb *still* can also take up several positions in a sentence. It can substitute for *yet* when referring to possibility.

She may still decide to go.

The only real difference here is that *yet* (9) sounds slightly more formal.

First can appear with or without a suffix (*-ly*). It also demonstrates great mobility in a sentence.

They <u>first</u> need to read the instructions.   <u>First,</u> they need to read the instructions.

They need to <u>first</u> read the instructions.   They need to read the instructions <u>first</u>.

39
When an adverb has a negative influence

There are several ways to create negation in a sentence. The terms *not, none* and *no* are conventional means.

> *The employee was (not) clear about her role in the meeting.* (1)

Sometimes a negative prefix is available.

> *The employee was (un)clear about her role in the meeting.* (2)

Not cannot occur with main verbs without the assistance of an auxiliary or modal (3). The exception is when the verb *to be* is the main verb in the sentence (as seen in (1)).

> **I not leave until Wednesday.* (3i)

> *I will not leave until Wednesday.*† (3ii)

—Some terms have a negative meaning or interpretation (see also example (6i) in **47**).

> *He denied this was the case.* (4)

Others (e.g. *ever* and *either*) have negative alternatives (*never* and *neither*). Consider also the phrases *a little* and *a few*, which take a negative reading when the articles are removed. In (5), the meaning is 'some' and the outcome is positive; while in (6), the meaning is 'hardly any' and the outcome is negative.

> *A few people signed up for the class* (5)

> *Few people signed up for the class* (6)

—Certain adverbs have a negative meaning, or at least a meaning that relates to near or relative negation.

> *They barely looked at each other the entire time.*† (7)

> *She rarely has time to work on her other projects.* (8)

An adverb or adverbial with a negative meaning can be placed in initial position for emphasis. Note the inversion of the subject and verb (see also **44**).

At no point did she think to inform her colleagues about this. (9)

Rarely have we seen such impressive results at this stage. (10)

Not can also begin a sentence in this way.

Not since the 1980s has there been such creative output. (11)

◆ ◆ ◆

(12i) They deliberately didn't change the order.

(12ii) They didn't deliberately change the order.

(13i) He very smartly didn't glance at the examiner.

(13ii) He didn't glance at the examiner very smartly.

(14) I know not what I do.

Student enquiry: I am struggling to understand the difference between the two sets of sentences (12, 13). Is there a particular rule for where to place the adverb in a negative statement? And in (14), *not* is used with a main verb but there is no auxiliary or modal auxiliary alongside it, which is contrary to the guidelines.

Explanation

The difference in meaning between the sets of examples in (12) and (13) relates to the extent or the scope of the negation in each sentence. When adverbs follow the negative term (which in these examples is *didn't*), then they are said to be included in or influenced by the negation. If they come before the negative term, then they are outside of it. The part underlined is the scope or extent of the negation.

They deliberately didn't change the order. (12i)

They didn't deliberately change the order. (12ii)

He very smartly didn't glance at the examiner. (13i)

He didn't glance at the examiner very smartly. (13ii)

It follows, then, that the position will affect the meaning of the sentence.

(12i) = They meant to keep the order the way it was, and they did.

(12ii) = They changed the order but did not mean to change it.

(13i) = He made sure not to glance at the examiner.

(13ii) = He deliberately glanced at the examiner hoping that the examiner would not see him looking but did not manage to achieve this.

And (14) is an example of a literary formal English or older English style where main verbs precede *not* without the need for an auxiliary verb in the sentence.

And another thing . . . 39

Modal verbs are often outside of the negation range. One exception is when *may* is used as a command or directive.

You may not change the order.†

Otherwise, it occurs outside the negation and this, naturally, will alter the meaning. With the addition of a clause it is no longer a command. It is now a suggestion or recommendation. Note the extent of the underlined part as well.

You may not change the order but at least consider the timings.†

40
To boldly split the infinitive

We have seen that adverbs can take up numerous positions in a sentence. Some are able to appear at the beginning, in the middle, or at the end of a clause. And they do not have to directly precede or follow the verb they are modifying. An object can sit between the verb and the adverb (1i). However, an adverb cannot go between a verb and its object (1ii).

We used the assistants effectively during this stage. (1i)

*We used effectively the assistants during this stage. (1ii)

Typically though, the adverb will occur directly before (2) or after (3) the verb.

They often accept students who have failed elsewhere. (2)

She reads aimlessly and fails to retain information. (3)

—As seen in **38**, adverbs can be fronted for emphasis, and this leads to inversion of the subject and verb.

Once the manager entered, out went the relaxed atmosphere and in came the tense exchanges. (4)

We had been waiting around half an hour when along came a marshal. (5)

—Adverbs appearing in the initial position of a sentence and separated from the main clause by a comma relate to the whole of the clause; in other words, they influence or modify the rest of the sentence. They are therefore sometimes called sentence adverbs.

Controversially, this fine was increased and they were also told they had no grounds for appeal. (6)

—An adverb can be placed before or after the verb *to be*. When appearing before, it tends to put emphasis on the verb. The emphasis in (8) would be on *is*.

She is usually the last to know.† (7)

Yes, she usually is the last to know.† (8)

◆ ◆ ◆

(9) Student F looked to always ask the teacher first.

(10i) I decided to swiftly remove this student from the situation.

Student enquiry: In English, you are not supposed to split an infinitive phrase and yet in (9) and (10i) the adverb is placed between the *to* and the verb. Has this been done in error?

Explanation

Along with never finishing a sentence with a preposition (see **34**), not splitting up an infinitive is impractical and unnecessary advice that can generally be ignored. The reason is that a natural place for the adverb is directly before the verb. In (9), there is an argument that *always* could be positioned elsewhere, but it is common usage for this adverb to occur between the two elements, especially when listing a set of goals or resolutions.

To always show empathy with my colleagues. (11)

To always find time to discuss an issue with my team. (12)

The consideration should not be whether the two elements have been split up but that the adverb has been placed in the appropriate phrase or clause.

In (10i) the adverb works well in this position, as it relates to the removing of the student. If the infinitive was not split, then the adverb might refer to the decision being made swiftly (*I swiftly decided*) rather than the action of the removal being swift, which may not have been the writer's intention. Otherwise, it would have to be placed after the object.

I decided to remove this student swiftly from the situation. (10ii)

Here is the example again but slightly modified.

After some minutes, I decided to swiftly remove the final letter before anyone noticed. (13i)

Time has been taken over the decision, so *swiftly decided* would be inappropriate. And it would also contradict the meaning if the adverb occurred directly before the infinitive phrase (*decided swiftly to remove . . .*).

It cannot come directly after the verb (**I decided to remove swiftly . . .*) and coming after the object can sometimes leave the adverb appearing to have more of a relationship with the subsequent phrase than with the verb

I decided to remove the final letter swiftly before anyone noticed. (13ii)

There is nothing especially wrong with this option except that it is natural to link an -*ly* adverb with the term that follows, so instead of 'swiftly remove' we perceive 'swiftly before.'

And then there is (14), where a split infinitive is unavoidable.

ALPB are reporting that costs are <u>to more than triple</u> next year.   (14)

Clearly, then, splitting an infinitive is not a grammatical error that should be eliminated. Once you've considered the meaning of the sentence and assessed its structure and perhaps rhythm, you can then decide which position is suitable.

And another thing . . . 40

Splitting the infinitive can also take place in negative phrases.

He tried <u>to not care</u> about this, but it was proving difficult.

Compare: *He tried <u>not to care</u> about this, but it was proving difficult.*

It is perhaps less appropriate here because it could be argued that the sentence reads and flows better without the split. The only reason for choosing the first example would be to create a kind of dramatic emphasis (to put emphasis on the negative, the 'not caring'). This is likely to be applied in fiction and reflective writing.

Understanding 33–40

Note: some questions may have more than one correct answer. Some questions may have no correct or no incorrect answers.

33. A. In which of these sentences are you NOT able to 'front' the preposition?

Which school did he study at?   What did he do that for?

What station was it at?

B. Which preposition should follow the term *likelihood*?

It will depend on the context.   in   on   of

34. A. Which of these participles can be used attributively?

found   afraid   sole

B. Which position is an adjective NOT able to occupy in a sentence?

directly after a noun   directly after a verb   directly before a noun

35. A. Which of these modifiers would come first if they were all modifying the same head noun in a sentence?

large   three   new

B. When would you NOT use a comma to split up adjectives?

when the adjectives are of the same type/category

when the adjectives might otherwise lead to ambiguity

when the adjectives are of different types/categories

36. A. Which of the following terms is NOT a comparative phrase?

upper   lower   more simple

B. Which of the following adjectives can take either an inflection or *more* for their comparative?

simple   honest   quiet   selfish

37. A. Which of these word classes can adverbs modify?

Other adverbs   adjectives   verbs

B. Which of the following words can be both an adjective and an adverb?

late   wrong   daily   old

38. A. In which position(s) can the time adverb *later* appear in a sentence?

after the main verb   at the beginning   at the end

B. Which of these is NOT true about the time adverb *yet*?

It cannot occur in negative sentences.   It often appears after an auxiliary.

It can appear at the beginning, in the middle and at the end of a sentence.

39. A. When an adverb follows a negative term, it . . .

is not influenced by the negation.   is influenced by the negation.

is representative of an older literary style.

B. Which is the most suitable phrase to indicate that there was not much interest?

Fewer people signed up.   Few people signed up.

A few people signed up.

40. A. What is the phrase *to always make* considered an example of?

a split infinitive   a comparative construction   a dangling modifier

B. What happens when an adverb is fronted for emphasis?

The infinitive will be split.   The subject and verb may be inverted.

The sentence will take on a negative meaning.

D. SUBJECT, CLAUSES, AND QUESTIONS

41
The topic is the subject

As a standard description, most reference books state that the subject of a sentence will be a person, place or thing in the form of a noun or noun phrase. They'll also likely assert that the subject will be what the sentence is about, i.e. its topic. We can clearly identify the subjects in (1) and (2) and recognise that information is being provided about them.

The issue has not yet been resolved. (1)

I added two more countries to my sample. (2)

But next, we have an infinitive verb form (3), a subordinate clause (4), and a direct quote (5) as subjects—going against these general guidelines.

To question the teacher is seen as disrespectful. (3)

Why he is doing this is anybody's guess.† (4)

'We don't wish to make drastic changes' was a common expression used. (5)

And in (6), *anyone* is the subject. It is questionable whether this pronoun can be considered the topic or that we are receiving information about it. The principal information is the changing of status.

Anyone can change their status. (6)

In (7) the reference is generic and the pronoun *you* performs the role of subject. But this sentence is about skating, the main square and the time of year—everything apart from the subject!

In winter, you can skate in the main square. (7)

◆ ◆ ◆

(8) Nobody has seen this latest design.

(9) Equally vague are these obligations.

(10) Quietly is how it should be done.

(11) Move your things!†

Student enquiry: What is the subject of the sentence in (8)? I thought perhaps it was *nobody*, but could it be the noun phrase *latest design*? And in (9), again, I cannot identify a subject. For (10), I am wondering whether an adverb (*Quietly*) can function as the subject of a sentence. And I cannot identify a subject at all in (11).

Explanation

(8) is a good example of a sentence having no real contender for actor, but *nobody* is indeed the subject. The topic would be regarded as *the latest design* and the fact that no one has seen it.

The subject in (9) is *these obligations* and it has been placed at the end to allow the complement *equally vague* to be fronted. Note also the subject-verb inversion and the fact that the verb is plural to agree with the subject.

There could be debate over the identity of the subject in (10). Some might argue that the adverb *quietly* is the subject of the sentence (a function that an adverb would never normally hold), while others would recognise *it* as the true subject, whatever *it* might be. But bear in mind that this would not be classed as a dummy subject (see **And another thing** below); we are just unaware what the pronoun is referring to, having only been given a short extract to work from.

(11) is an imperative, and in these types of sentence the subject can be implied.

And another thing . . . 41

A sentence may also contain what is known as a 'dummy' subject (see **48** and **49**).

> *It is clear that problems exist.*

In this instance, *it* fills in as the subject, but there is no real meaning attached to it. This serves as another example of a subject not providing the topic or any real information to the reader (*there* is also commonly used as a dummy; see **48**).

42
Although they look like main clauses . . .

Main (independent) clauses represent complete thoughts and therefore can stand on their own as sentences.

I did not recognise her at the function. (1)

In contrast, subordinate (dependent) clauses are not considered full sentences, only fragments, and therefore cannot exist independently. The clause below (2) requires a comma and further information, not a full stop.

*Although I had seen her before. (2)

When a main clause is attached to (2), the sentence becomes complete.

Although I had seen her before, I did not recognise her at the function. (3)

Commas will separate these clauses when the sentence begins with a subordinate clause (4). If the sentence opens with a main clause (5), then a comma is only required if the connecting word is one of contrast or concession, such as *unless* and *whereas* (6).

When they reach question four, the participants can talk. (4)

The participants can talk when they have reached question four. (5)

The participants can talk, unless they have been told they cannot. (6)

—Main clauses contain finite verbs, meaning that they show tense (7). Verb forms that do not show tense (known as non-finite verbs) are gerunds, infinitives and participles (8). Note that the underlined part in (7) represents a main clause (i.e. a complete thought) and could stand on its own. The underlined part in (8), however, is subordinate and requires additional content, i.e. a tensed or finite verb, for it to represent a sentence.

<u>They finished</u> the course yesterday.† (7)

<u>Before finishing</u>, I must mention some colleagues who have helped me.† (8)

◆ ◆ ◆

(9) The more you change, the more you stay the same.

(10) Not to panic. This can be resolved quickly.†

Student enquiry: I have been trying to identify which is the main clause and which is the subordinate clause in (9). In (10), it seems to me as though there are two main clauses, because they are both complete sentences; yet, the first clause (*Not to panic*) does not contain a finite verb, which then causes me to doubt this and wonder why it has a full stop after it.

Explanation

Example (9) is a comparative correlative sentence. It initially appears as though the first clause is the dependent or subordinate one. In fact, neither is a main clause, as neither can stand without the other. The two clauses are often reversible (you can place the second clause in the initial position), but this will usually affect the meaning.

(10) does feature two main clauses, the first one containing a non-finite verb. Along with certain concise phrases (*Good to know*) and questions (*Why now?*) this is a rare exception to the rule that states every sentence must contain a finite verb (see also **And another thing**).

And another thing . . . 42

Headline writers often ignore the grammar conventions of the language and use non-finite main clauses, where ellipsis (see **Glossary**) of the auxiliary produces an attention-grabbing and incisive style.

President to resign next week

Workers sent for retraining

43
When discussing dangling . . .

An absolute phrase or clause adds information to a sentence but does so without being directly connected to the other clause(s). It modifies the main clause and can appear at the beginning (1), in the middle (2) or at the end of a sentence (3). Note the punctuation.

> *The meeting nearly over*, Jane began to pack away her things. (1)

> An operative, *when trained*, will have access to these systems. (2)

> The participant turned left and followed the road, *led by the signal on the device*. (3)

There is a disconnection between the absolute clause and the other clause(s), set apart as it is by a comma or commas, with often some form of ellipsis. In (3), it is the omission of the participle (*being*).

Despite the lack of a union, there is a semantic relation between the clauses. But sometimes these phrases can be used erroneously, wherein they fail to correspond with the information in the next or the previous part. Participles are the culprits here, and they are said to be dangling:

> **Fixing the problem*, the device soon began to function effectively. (4)

> **Being late*, the class had already begun. (5)

Often the issue is the lack of an actor carrying out the action. We have here two inanimate elements (*a device* and *a class*). In (4), the device is seemingly fixing the problem itself. In (5) we are not told who was late, just that the class had begun. And in (6i), an infinitive phrase creates the same issue but in a subtler way.

> *To create the mould*, the sheet was heated and then stretched out. (6i)

This may appear a reasonable sentence grammatically because it is a passive construction and the writer has no wish to identify those responsible for carrying out the process; however, when a sentence begins with an infinitive phrase it will require an actor, or we will have a similar problem to the one the participles created in (4) and (5). To resolve this issue, the sentence could contain a pronoun

(6ii) from which it will gain an actor to carry out the action. Or, it could be turned into an imperative (6iii), wherein it will take on the form of a set of instructions.

> *To create the mould, we heated the sheet and then stretched it out.*   (6ii)

> *To create the mould, heat the sheet and then stretch it out.*   (6iii)

◆ ◆ ◆

(7) Generally speaking, the problem is a rural one.

(8) When arriving at the conference, a supervisor will be on hand to answer any questions.

Student enquiry: It looks to me like (7) and (8) have dangling participles. I guess the writer is the one speaking generally in (7), but the same problem seems to be occurring where there is a disconnection between the clauses. And in (8), there is no information about who is arriving at the conference. I thought this was supposed to be avoided in writing.

Explanation

Examples (7) and (8) could be considered to contain dangling participles. *Generally speaking* in (7) is a common expression that does seem to violate the principles. Of greater concern is the vagueness of the term, though. Certainly, in academic writing this is not ideal. A similar expression, *strictly speaking*, also tends to dangle but at least has a more defined meaning.

(8) is another example of a dangling participle but is perhaps more acceptable because the unexpressed subject is an indefinite one and the sentence is in the form of a directive. Advice is being offered for when visiting a conference. A similar example is this extract from a business guide providing some pointers to the reader.

> *When sitting in these meetings, contribute to the discussion by posing a question.*   (9)

So, directives or instructions may well have dangling elements. And when the speaker/writer or listener/reader is considered the subject (as seen in (7) and (8) respectively), these phrases are more acceptable.

> *Looking at this objectively, you only have one course of action.*   (10)

This disconnection between the subject and the initial clause can also be observed when the sentence begins with the prepositions *regarding*, *following* or *considering*.

Following the conference, we went to recheck our findings.   (11)

Regarding the sample, we have yet to identify key age groups.   (12)

And another thing . . . 43

Absolute phrases might not actually contain a verb. As stated earlier, the information within the phrase will relate (or refer) in some way to the subject in the main clause.

Secure in this knowledge, he could now show them how the device worked in a real-world scenario.

44
Subject and verb switching

The textbook example of the subject and the verb switching places is in forming questions. Statements in English are in the order of subject + verb (1i), and for questions this is inverted (1ii).

> _You are_ working hard on this project.† (1i)

> _Are you_ working hard on this project? † (1ii)

But this does not apply for all questions. If a sentence begins with an interrogative word and this word is the subject, then there will be no inversion.

> _Who can read this easily?_ † (2)

—In reality, inversion occurs frequently in English and is often unrelated to asking questions. Notice in the exchanges in (3) and (4) that the short responses invert the subject and verb from the initial statements to show agreement.

> _I will visit Harbin in November. So will I._† (3)

> _I have never seen this sort of reaction before. Neither have I._† (4)

Conditional clauses (5, 6) and the subjunctive mood (7) (see **24** and **25**) also produce inverted forms (verb + subject).

> _Should you reconsider_, we could leave in the morning. (5)

> _Had this happened earlier_, the outcome would have been very different. (6)

> _Were I to be tested now_, there is no way I would pass. (7)

And recall in **23** that inversion can take place when reporting speech.

> _'I can't really discuss that'_, _admitted the governor_. (8)

◆ ◆ ◆

(9) Not only did they solve the algorithm, but they also invented a new form of computation.

(10) Only with the support of the other parties can the scheme be implemented.

Student enquiry: As it is not a question, shouldn't (9) begin with *Not only they did . . . ?* And in (10), the second part of the sentence seems like a question, not a statement. I would have expected it written . . . *Only with the support of the other parties the scheme can be implemented.*

Explanation

When *not* begins a sentence, it can create inversion. This is evident in the first part of (9) where *they* and *did* are inverted. The form of the sentence is *not only . . . but also.* And in this next example, *not until* leads to inversion of the second part of the sentence.

> *Not until I looked at the plans <u>did I</u> realise the enormity of the task.*   (11)

(10) is a conditional beginning *Only with.* This construction leads to inversion of the second part of the sentence as well. This is also true of sentences beginning *Only if.*

> *Only if they leave now <u>will they</u> be able to catch the train.*   (12)

Notice that the second part of (12) would, ordinarily, be a question. And this was the essence of the enquiry relating to (10) above.

> *Will they be able to catch the train?*

And another thing . . . 44

Recall from **39** that when adverbs are positioned initially, they can produce inversion. The purpose of the fronting is to add emphasis.

> <u>*Little did I*</u> *imagine when I arrived there that I would be leading them within two years.*

> <u>*Rarely have we*</u> *seen such a spirited performance from a novice.*

45
A positive clause, a positive tag

Tag questions occur as attached clauses and are produced through ellipsis of the main clause. In (1), the tag question is a shortened form of *Can you work out how to make this smaller?*

I can't work out how to make this smaller; can you? † (1)

They often represent a need for approval or confirmation.

We can't go this way, can we? † (2)

I would choose the third option; wouldn't you? † (3)

Notice in (2) and (3) that when the modal in the declarative clause is negative, the modal in the tag question is affirmative (positive) and vice versa. The tag is being used to verify that the listener agrees with the assertion.

I do think we need to give this more thought; don't you? † (4)

—A modal verb may not always appear in the initial or declarative clause. In (5), the lack of a modal gives authority and sternness to the directive. Including a tag provides a degree of politeness.

Open that file for me, would you? † (5)

—Intonation can be crucial when interpreting what has been said. In (6), rising intonation implies there is some doubt in the speaker's mind that the person is going.

You are going, aren't you? † (6)

Falling intonation on the tag question would imply that the speaker is merely confirming and expects the person to be going.

These examples suggest that a tag question will serve to weaken an assertion; but in (7), the tag demonstrates confidence and that the speaker has control of the conversation.

Just concentrate on the task I have given you, will you? † (7)

◆ ◆ ◆

(8) You have finally changed the logo, have you?†

(9) They are going ahead with it then, are they?†

Student enquiry: In (8) and (9), the auxiliaries of the tag questions are in the same form (positive) as those in the main clauses. I thought the two parts had to have different forms. Shouldn't there be negative tags in (8) and (9) so they are the opposite of the auxiliaries in the main clauses? (i.e. *you have . . . haven't you?* / *they are . . . aren't they?*)

Explanation

The tag question does not have to be in the opposite form to the declarative statement that precedes it. Both can be positive. One outcome of this is a tag with a sarcastic (8) or a mildly disapproving (9) tone to it. So, in (8) the positive tag implies that the speaker is sarcastically thankful that something has finally been done. It would likely also have rising intonation. If the tag was negative (*You have finally changed the logo, haven't you?*), it would be an enquiry in the hope that something has been done. Even though two positive elements do not always result in sarcasm or disapproval, there is often a judgemental element to it. The intonation in (9), then, on the tag question *are they?* could be rising (indicating pleasant surprise or surprised disappointment) or be falling (resigned disappointment)

And another thing . . . 45

When there is no modal/auxiliary in the declarative clause, the verb *to do* can step in and occupy the tag part.

I deleted the file, did I? †

46
You know how to respond to this question, do you?

A response to a tag question could be in the form of simply repeating the modal/auxiliary.

I would change that straight away; wouldn't you? †

I would.† (1)

Or it could be a simple yes or no.

I would change that straight away; wouldn't you? †

Yes.† (2)

Naturally, these responses can be in the negative (*I wouldn't/No*). The interpretation of the question in the tag part and the response to it are generally straightforward matters. But sometimes the answer will appear to have no connection to the question (i.e. the reply is neither yes or no nor a repeat of the modal) though the response can still be understood.

I am going to the office party; are you? †

Everyone goes to this party.†   (meaning *of course I am going*) (3)

And for questions such as those found in (4), there may be ambiguity regarding both intention and response (see also **student enquiry**).

Are you going? † (4i)

Aren't you going? † (4ii)

The affirmative *Are you going?* has a neutral inference and implies that the speaker has received no information about whether the person is going or not. The negative *Aren't you going?* could imply either that the speaker thought the person was going and may now have information to the contrary, or just that the person should be going for whatever reason.

◆ ◆ ◆

(4i) Are you going?†

(4ii) Aren't you going?†

Student enquiry: I am uncertain as to the suitable responses for (4i) and (4ii). For instance, If I am going to the event, I know that I should respond affirmatively in (4i) and if I am not, then I say *no*. But how would I respond to the question that is set up negatively (4ii)? If I am not going, should I say yes or no?

Explanation

Responding to a negatively framed question is something people whose first language is not English can struggle with. And the issue is not just with how to respond but also how to interpret that response. Even for English speakers, there may be some confusion if the reply to (4ii) provides no further information (information such as *No, I am not*). For these particular examples, the problem mainly occurs when the responder answers in the affirmative (*Yes*) to (4ii). The assumption of the responder may be that because the question was negatively framed, then the correct response to not going would be to agree with the nature of the question and reply with *yes*. But this would be ambiguous for the person asking the question. They would not then know whether the person was going or not. Most English speakers would therefore reply either *No* or *Yes, I am going*.

Here is another example with a tag and the available responses.

You didn't like it, did you? †

If you didn't like it: *No* or *No, I didn't*.†

If you did like it: *No, I did like it* or *Yes, I did like it*.†

Note that, interestingly, for an affirmative answer to a negative question, it is possible to answer either *yes* or *no* as long as additional confirmatory information is provided.

And another thing . . . 46

A declarative question appears to be a statement but is in fact an enquiry that uses rising intonation. Without this intonation, the listener would simply assume it to be a statement. It is often elliptical in form, missing the interrogative term.

She applied for the job? †

Notice that the subject comes before the verb as it would in a statement.

Somebody's here? †

In this next example, the declarative question is being used to confirm the truth of a previous utterance.

He changes his password every day.†

He changes it every day? †

47
Unanswered questions

There are instances when a question is posed without any expectation that it will be answered. These questions are called rhetorical. One reason for this type of question is that the person asking is planning on providing the answer.

And how do we deal with this? By working as a team. (1)

Equally, the answer may be so obvious it does not require a response.

Who is going to bother doing that? † *(nobody)* (2)

What are they like? † *(silly/unconventional)* (3)

Rhetorical questions may just be everyday phrases that have the structure of questions but either warrant no reply or the reply matches the original utterance. In (4), a simple greeting with the equivalence of hello is offered and then repeated before a standard question is asked.

Alright?

How's it going?

Did you watch that documentary? † (4)

In (5), we have what appears to be an accusation which may or may not wish to be answered by the accused.

How could you? † (5)

Interestingly, a positively framed rhetorical question (6i) may have a negative meaning and vice versa.

Did I say you could do it overnight? † (meaning: I didn't say you could . . .) (6i)

Didn't I say you could do it overnight? † (meaning: I said you could . . .) (6ii)

This occurs in standard questions too. Here in (7), the negatively framed *I don't suppose you* is simply a polite substitute for *Do you*.

I don't suppose you have a pen? (7)

As (6i) demonstrates, we can have a semantically negative question with no indication of this negativity from the syntax (for instance, the question fails to include *not*). In (8), the negative meaning is implied and the tone of voice will likely reveal the feelings of the speaker.

Does he always have to say something? †   (8)

◆ ◆ ◆

(9) They expect you to have a licence for that, though.

How would they even know?†

(10) She asked how we should get there.†

(11) I am thinking about how this is going to work.†

Student enquiry: Is the respondent in (9) being rhetorical, or can this be considered a regular question requiring an answer? I am also unclear why (10) and (11) do not finish in question marks, as they both contain the question adverb *how*. Do they require answering?

Explanation

(9) is likely to be a rhetorical response, the implication being that there is no practical way of checking whether someone has obtained a licence. If the listener is unaware of the rhetorical nature, then they would answer with *They wouldn't*.

The presence of an interrogative word does not necessarily indicate that the utterance is a question. (10) and (11) feature interrogative terms but are statements that contain embedded questions. (10) is an example of reported speech.

A common error is to reverse the subject-verb order for an embedded question to comply with the normal form of a question.

*She asked how should we get there.

She asked how we should get there.†

*I am thinking about how is this going to work.

I am thinking about how this is going to work.†

But embedded questions follow the regular pattern of statements.

The embedded form may also occur within questions. And this form adds politeness to the enquiry.

Would you be able to tell me <u>where the library is?</u> †   (12i)

Compare the underlined part of (12i) with the regular question form.

Where is the library? †   (12ii)

And another thing . . . 47

Similarly, exclamatory questions may require neither an answer nor a question mark. Usually an exclamation mark will do.

Hasn't he improved! †

Sometimes a question mark is more practical.

What is that about? †

Using both an exclamation mark and a question mark is unwarranted and is only really used in informal texts for reporting dialogue. The practice should be avoided altogether in any formal or academic written work.

How excessive is that?! †

48
A word with no meaning

When a sentence cannot conveniently follow on from the previous sentence, discussion or theme, it may require what is known as a 'dummy' subject to initiate things (see also **41** and **49**). A common method for doing this is to use *there* with the verb *to be* as illustrated in (1) and (2).

There should be one more person in each group. (1)

There was a difference of opinion when the two met in June. (2)

Perhaps the most recognisable use of *there* is as a demonstrative to indicate the location or position of an object or event relative to the speaker. *There* can also be used as a demonstrative adverb (3).

The headquarters is just over there.† (3)

But *there* does not indicate location in (1) or (2), and in (4) it refers to the mere existence of something.

There was a strange atmosphere. (4)

In this type of sentence *there* plays the subject role. Sometimes, dummy *there* is unavoidable or at least the simplest and most effective way of expressing the point.

There is a problem with page 20. (5)

It also occurs in tag questions as the subject.

There was an issue, wasn't there? † (6)

Here in (7), it is the head of an infinitive clause.

We don't want there to be any arguments.† (7)

—Dummy *there* appears to create subject-verb inversion in (8ii) (although there is no inversion because *there* has become the subject). Note also that in this example the accompanying verb is not a form of *to be* (see **And another thing**).

A blackbird appeared from behind one of our equipment bags. (8i)

There appeared a blackbird from behind one of our equipment bags. (8ii)

One final point regarding dummy *there* is that a tense change can occur over the course of the sentence.

There <u>are</u> some objects that <u>were</u> repainted prior to the exhibition. (9)

◆ ◆ ◆

(10) There was a sourcebook and an instructional manual on the desk.

(11) There seems to be three viewpoints on this matter.

(12) It is her party next week.†

(13) It is sunny at the moment here.†

Student enquiry: I find it strange that (10) and (11) contain singular verb forms when the references (*sourcebook and manual / three viewpoints*) are clearly plural. Does this have anything to do with the dummy subject at the beginning?

And it seems to me as though *it* serves the same purpose as *there* in being a dummy subject because in (12) and (13) it does not have any meaning and does not appear to refer to anything.

Explanation

As *there* is a 'dummy' form with no real reference attached to it, you would expect the subsequent verb and noun phrase to follow the rules regarding subject-verb agreement as (14) does with a plural verb and plural noun phrase.

There <u>are three reports</u> left to read.† (14)

However, there are instances when it is either logical or simply common usage for writers, and especially speakers, to use a singular verb form despite a plural noun phrase appearing in the sentence. In (10) there are two items being referred to, but the dummy subject allows a singular verb. Compare (10) with another version (15) that omits the opening phrase. The expected plural verb is now employed.

A sourcebook and an instructional manual <u>were</u> on the desk. (15)

Another occasion in which an unexpected singular verb can be seen is when *there* is followed by catenative verbs such as *seem* and *appear*. This is the explanation for (11).

A further occasion is when the contraction *there's* is used.

There's some issues that we will need to address.†   (*There is*) (16)

(12) and (13) do contain dummy operators, with *It* standing in as the subject in these sentences. As with *there*, *it* has no real meaning or purpose other than providing a subject. Sentences with dummy *it* usually relate to time, distance or the weather. These next two examples help to demonstrate how *it* can be used to refer to something mentioned previously (in (17) this is a parcel) and where it has no real reference (18).

> *We need to get to the office before it gets there.*† (17)

> *We need to get to the office before it gets too late.*† (18)

Another situation in which *it* lacks any lexical content is (19), where it appears as an empty object alongside a complement and a clause.

> *They make it confusing to understand how the device actually works.* (19)

And another thing . . . 48

In literary and poetic texts, *there* can be used with verbs other than *be*.

> *There sits among the heath a small burial stone.*

49
The sentence that makes you wait

Some opening clauses are designed to bring a later point or discussion into focus. These clauses create what are known as cleft sentences. In (1i), the cleft creates a build-up before the result is announced that is absent in (1ii).

The candidate who has achieved the highest mark is Jonathon. (1i)

Jonathon has achieved the highest mark. (1ii)

In (2), the cleft is in the form of 'It + be + point of emphasis + clause'.

It was my supervisor who told me to add another theme to chapter four. (2)

These clefts can be linked with relative clauses (see **Glossary**) that begin with *who, that* or *when.*

It is the second report that will arrive next week.† (3)

It was six weeks ago when I changed the information on the website.† (4)

◆ ◆ ◆

(5) It is the tutors who are being interviewed last.

(6) It's the macros that are causing the most problems.

Student enquiry: I recognise (5) and (6) as cleft sentences, but I am not sure how plural nouns and verbs can be used if the subject is the singular pronoun *it.* Doesn't this go against subject-verb agreement?

Explanation

In cleft sentences, the role of *It* is to help anticipate something. Because it is only really the subject in a syntactic sense, there are no restrictions on, say, whether it can be followed by a singular noun phrase or a plural one.

It is the tutor/tutors who is/are going too slowly, not me.† (7)

Essentially, dummy *it* and cleft *it* should not be recognised in the same way as the singular pronoun *it*. The verb in the relative clause will simply agree with the noun phrase and not with *it*, and in (5) and (6) we can see plural verb forms agreeing with the plural nouns *tutors* and *macros*.

And another thing . . . 49

There is also a related form that is known as the pseudo-cleft. Pseudo-cleft sentences usually begin with *what*, and the element being emphasised comes after the relative clause. In these next examples, the emphasis is placed on the noun phrase at the end.

What works better is a social media post.

What this leads to is a safe environment.

But it is possible to reverse the subject and complement in a pseudo-cleft.

A social media post is what works better.

A safe environment is what this leads to.

50
Expanding on the contraction

As well as indicating possession, apostrophes can be employed to substitute for the missing words in a contraction.

He's the oldest member of the team. (1)

Here, the apostrophe represents the missing letter *i* of the phrase *He is*. In (2), it stands in for *ha* in the phrase *She had*.

She'd better not go without me.† (2)

She'd can also signify *she would*.

She'd do that as well, wouldn't she? † (3)

There are a few other contractions that can represent more than one modal/auxiliary.

he'll—he will / he shall   I'd—I had / I would   It's—It is / It has

—The characteristic mistake in this area is confusing the determiner *its* with the contraction of *it is*.

*We will try to find it's simplest form. (4i)

We will try to find its simplest form. (4ii)

—Informally, contractions can be used on nouns to substitute for *is* or *has*.

The textbook's telling us to switch the operators around.† (5)

◆ ◆ ◆

(6) I won't change the setting.†

(7) Won't this change the setting?†

Student enquiry: I know that *won't* stands for *will not* and in (6), the contracted form can be replaced by *will not*. But in (7) I realise that you cannot say *will not this*, so what does *won't* represent here?

Explanation

(6) is a statement in which *won't* is equivalent to *will not*. However, in interrogatives (questions) *won't* is not considered a substitute for *will not*. In (7), which is an interrogative, *Won't this* is equivalent instead to *Will this not*.

Compare this with (8).

   This won't change the setting, will it?   (*This will not change . . .*)   (8)

Because *won't* is in the main clause and it is a statement, there is equivalence between *won't* and *will not*. The interrogative is only in the tag part and so has no bearing on things.

Another feature of *won't* is that, along with other negative contractions, it is able to end a sentence (9). Most affirmative contractions cannot be used in the final position (where ellipsis will be taking place).

   I will remember, but he won't.†   (9)

   We haven't got our questionnaires yet, but they have.†   (10)

   *We haven't got our questionnaires yet, but they've.

   They wouldn't ask questions, but we would.†   (11)

   *They wouldn't ask questions, but we'd.

And another thing . . . 50

When *let us* has the meaning of *allow us* or *permit us*, it cannot be contracted.

   Let us use this tomorrow and we can return the favour on Friday.†

   Let us find out for ourselves.†

Only the inclusive (me and you) imperative form of *let us* can be contracted. The second example means *allow us to find out for ourselves* (i.e. *do not tell us*). If we change this to an instruction or a suggestion, then the contraction can be employed.

   Let's find out for ourselves, shall we? †

Understanding 41–50

Note: some questions may have more than one correct answer. Some questions may have no correct or no incorrect answers.

41. A. What is the subject in the sentence *Equally vague are their values*?

equally vague   their values   their

B. In what instance might a subject NOT appear in a sentence?

when it is an imperative   when the sentence is passive

when the sentence contains an indefinite pronoun

42. A. What do the phrases *good to know, not to panic, president to marry* have in common?

They are all interrogatives.   They do not contain a finite verb.

They do not contain a subject.

B. What do headline writers sometimes do?

omit the subject   omit a direct object   omit a tensed verb form

43. A. The sentence *Being late, the class had already begun* contains what?

a superlative   a dangling participle   a split infinitive

B. Which of these comments about absolute phrases is true?

They don't have to contain a verb.   They always contain instructions.

They always appear at the beginning of a sentence.

44. A. When might you see the subject and verb switching places?

in a sentence that ends in *not*   in a conditional clause

in an embedded question

B. Complete the sentence: *Not only did I go . . .*

but also I spoke about my experiences.

I also spoke about my experiences.

but I also spoke about my experiences.

45. A. A positive statement followed by a positive tag could sound what?

professional   sarcastic   supportive

B. *You are going, aren't you?* When asking this question, to indicate that you consider them to be going you should NOT use:

neutral intonation   rising intonation   falling intonation

46. A. Which of the following is NOT a characteristic of a declarative question?

It asks a question.   It requires rising intonation.

It requires an exclamation mark.

B. Which of the following would be an ambiguous response to the question *Didn't you like it?*

Yes, I did.   No, I did.   Yes   No

47. A. What type of question does the sentence *Would you be able to tell me where the library is?* contain?

exclamatory   rhetorical   embedded

B. Which of these positively framed questions has a negative connotation?

Could you see that from there?   Could you move that over here?

Could it be any clearer?

48. A. In which of these sentences is *there* being used as a dummy subject?

There they are, by the office.   There was an issue earlier   It is there.

B. Which of the following can serve as a dummy subject?

there   it   here   their   do

49. A. Which of these is considered a pseudo-cleft sentence?

It is the first system that we like.   What we want is a voice.

The winner is Sophie.

B. Clefts can be linked by clauses that begin with which of these words?

who   then   that   since

50. A. In which sentence is *won't* NOT equivalent to *will not*?

Won't they stay?   I won't start just yet.   They won't need to.

B. Contractions may be used on nouns as a substitute for which of these words?

will   his   has   is

ANSWERS

Part A

1. A. beauty
   B. Shakespearian, Indian
2. A. ability
   B. unbounded
3. A. partridge
   B. 10,000 people
4. A. people
   B. The board is split on this issue.
5. A. systems (analyst)
   B. In compound adjectives the stress will fall on the second part.
6. A. the bus's engine
   B. They are usually informal in tone.
7. A. too small a target
   B. most
8. A. That was some lesson.
   B. All three types can be used.
9. A. The petition and later demonstration
   The hallway and lounge
   B. 7 or 9
10. A. We are conditioned to that.
    B. We do have confidence today.
11. A. They drive to work.
    B. his
12. A. all three
    B. A company changes its mind at stage three.
13. A. There is no set order.
    B. all three
14. A. when the listener knows the individual
    B. A Mr Andrews from accounts called.
15. A. in a headline/in a title
    B. President visited last year.

Part B

16. A. fair
    B. The initial syllable is stressed for the noun.
17. A. respond
    B. when the identity of the object is clear from the context
    when the verb appears in a conditional
18. A. wrote
    B. The present participle will end in –ing.
19. A. canceled
    B. trafficked
20. A. then I walk in
    B. all three
21. A. Sari used/uses these effects.
    B. Bonnie drives us to the meetings.
22. A. They had been checking this.
    B. past perfect progressive
23. A. when the utterance is still valid or relevant
    B. tell
24. A. When I am hungry, I eat.
    B. The main clause may or may not contain a future time reference.
25. A. If he were here
    B. The imperative mood is used for questions.
26. A. The student got removed eventually.

B. none of them
27. A. lack
    B. A passive clause must contain a participle.
    A passive clause cannot always be made active.
28. A. help
    B. They helped fix the machine.
    They helped to fix the machine.
29. A. I had an opportunity to go.
    B. They need not alter their approach.
30. A. She may be available.
    B. when indicating permission
    when issuing a refusal
31. A. to ask a question in the first person
    B. should
32. A. Do you have others?
    B. when not precedes a linking verb

Part C

33. A. What did he do that for?
    B. of
34. A. sole
    B. It can appear in all three positions.
35. A. three
    B. when the adjectives are of different types/categories
36. A. upper
    B. simple, quiet
37. A. all three
    B. late, wrong, daily
38. A. all three
    B. It cannot occur in negative sentences.
39. A. is influenced by the negation.
    B. Few people signed up.
40. A. a split infinitive
    B. The subject and verb may be inverted.

Part D

41. A. their values
    B. when it is an imperative
42. A. They do not contain a finite verb.
    B. omit a tensed verb form
43. A. a dangling participle
    B. They don't have to contain a verb.
44. A. in a conditional clause
    B. but I also spoke about my experiences.
45. A. sarcastic
    B. rising intonation
46. A. It requires an exclamation mark.
    B. Yes
47. A. embedded
    B. Could it be any clearer?
48. A. There was an issue earlier.
    B. there, it, do
49. A. What we want is a voice.
    B. who, that
50. A. Won't they stay?
    B. has, is

APPENDIX

Examples of key grammatical elements

Grammatical element	Example term
common noun	*building*
proper noun	*Sweden*
article	*an*
first person singular personal pronoun	*I*
first person plural personal pronoun	*we*
second person personal pronoun	*you*
third person singular personal pronoun	*it*
third person plural personal pronoun	*they*
possessive pronoun	*your*
possessive personal pronoun	*yours*
singular reflexive personal pronoun	*yourself*
plural reflexive personal pronoun	*yourselves*
indefinite pronoun	*nobody*
reflexive indefinite pronoun	*oneself*
wh- pronoun	*who*
wh- ever pronoun	*whoever*
singular determiner	*that*
plural determiner	*those*
wh- determiner	*which*
wh- determiner, genitive	*whose*
cardinal number	*one*
ordinal number	*second*
infinitive marker	*to*
base form -be	*be*
past tense -be	*was*
present participle -be	*being*
past participle -be	*been*

Grammatical element	Example term
base form -regular	*move*
past tense -regular	*moved*
present participle -regular	*moving*
past participle -regular	*moved*
modal auxiliary	*can*
coordinator	*and*
subordinating coordinator	*unless*
correlative coordinator	*neither/nor*
general preposition	*on*
general adjective	*strong*
general comparative adjective	*stronger*
general superlative adjective	*strongest*
attributive adjective	*long meeting*
predicative adjective	*meeting was long*
past participle used attributively	*a used car*
present participle used attributively	*a following wind*
genitive 's'	*company's*
degree adverb	*barely*
comparative degree adverb	*more*
superlative degree adverb	*most*

GLOSSARY

(1) = chapter number

adjunct (33): an optional part of a phrase or clause that, if removed, does not affect the rest of the phrase or clause. It can be distinguished from a complement which is a necessary part of the phrase/clause.

ambiguous (5, 9, 10, 15, 20, 27, 35, 46): having more than one potential interpretation; unclear.

appositives (6): two terms that are placed alongside each other and that share the same reference. The genitive form of apposition is an *of*-phrase that cannot be converted to the apostrophe form because the terms are parallel (e.g. *the month of February/*February's month*).

attributive (34): (relating to the position of an adjective or modifier) coming before the word that is being modified (e.g. *the broken window*).

catenative verb (28,48): a verb that can be followed directly by another verb form. Also known as a chain or chain-forming verb (e.g. *helped to see*). The second verb in the chain will be a non-finite verb.

collectivising (3,4): a phenomenon that occurs when naming certain animals (usually those hunted) and plants where a singular form is used despite the noun phrase requiring a plural (e.g. *We used some cauliflower as well*).

complement (15, 17, 26, 28, 29, 33, 34, 41, 48, 49): broadly speaking, complements can be considered anything coming after the verb and that is a necessary component of the sentence (i.e. it is a required element unlike an adjunct/adverbial which can be omitted).

SUBJECT	VERB	COMPLEMENT	ADJUNCT
The teacher	*is*	*ready*	*in the classroom.*

copular (17, 28, 34, 48): a verb that links the subject to the subject complement. The most commonly used copula is the verb *to be*. Another name for a copula verb is a linking verb.

ellipsis (17, 42, 43, 45, 46, 50): the omission of one or more words in a sentence, often for brevity or to avoid redundancy. Also the name of the three dots punctuation mark (. . .).

finite (27, 42): a term to describe tensed verb forms that have a subject and serve as the root for independent (main) clauses.

genitive (5, 6, 16): the case or a word in that case indicating ownership or possession. A word ending in 's to signify possession is said to be in the genitive form.

gradable (35, 36): an adjective that can vary in its degree or level of intensity and therefore one able to have comparative and superlative forms.

homonyms (16): words that have the same form (are spelled the same and pronounced the same) but are unrelated and have different meanings.

idiomatic (25, 33): relating to or characteristic of an idiom, an idiom being a sequence of words which has a different (usually figurative) meaning as a group from the meaning it would have if you assessed each word separately (e.g. *snowed under, be on the same page, off the hook*).

inflection (3, 5, 18, 36): a change to the form of words to indicate person, number, tense etc. The inflection *-er* is added to some adjectives to show that they are comparative forms.

irrealis (25): a grammatical mood that indicates that a certain situation or condition is unreal. Specifically, it is the use of *were* instead of *was* in a hypothetical phrase such as *If I were you*.

non-finite (42): a term that describes untensed verb forms such as infinitives, participles and gerunds that cannot occur as the root of an independent or main clause and appear in subordinate ones instead.

particles (33): a subset of adverbs/prepositions that act as a complement to the preceding word but do not take complements. They may have flexibility of position in relation to the direct object (e.g. *in* and *up* in the phrases *give in, give up*).

polysemes (16): words that have the same form (are spelled the same and pronounced the same) and have different but related meanings.

predicative (34): (relating to the position of an adjective or modifier) coming after a linking verb (e.g. *the window is broken*) and modifying the subject of that verb.

relative clause (33, 49): A type of subordinate clause that begins with a relative pronoun (*who, which, that, whose, where, when*) and modifies a noun or noun phrase. These clauses may be defining, in which case they add essential information about the noun phrase, or they may have a non-defining role where they provide additional but non-essential information about the noun phrase.

semantic: relating to meaning.

syncretism (20): a single form of a word fulfilling two different functions, the most common being the past form of a verb having the same spelling as the past participle. Some verbs (such as *put*) show additional syncretism with identical forms for the simple past, the simple present, and the past participle.

syntactic (noun–syntax): relating to form and the arrangement of words.

SUBJECT INDEX